THE
MITTEN
HAND
BOOK

THE
MITTEN
HANDBOOK

Knitting Recipes to Make Your Own   MARY SCOTT HUFF

ABRAMS | NEW YORK

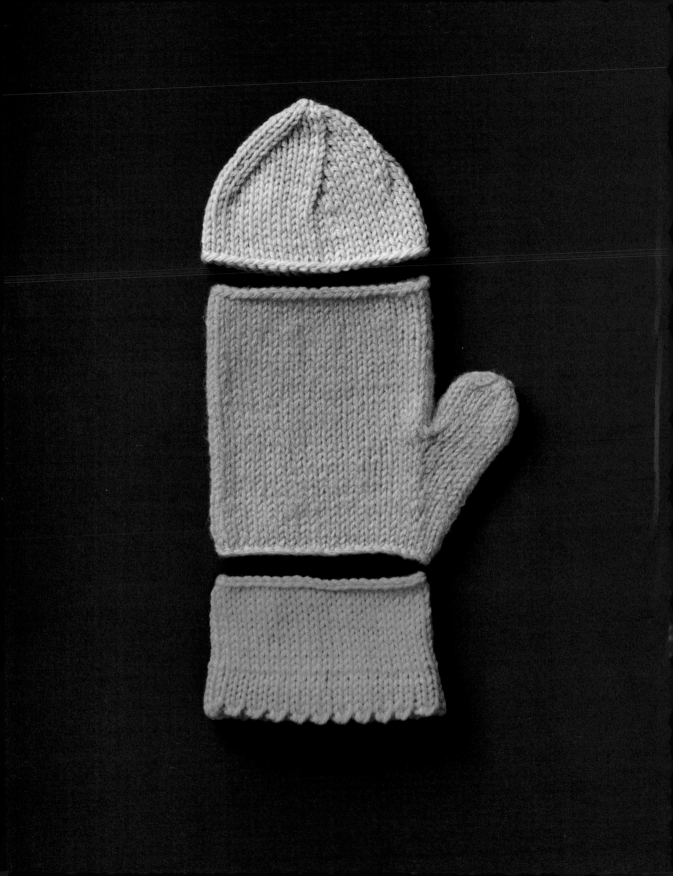

INTRODUCTION

This book was inspired by my knitting students, who asked me again and again to create a volume that would help them to knit mittens exactly the way they imagined them. They wanted a book that would act as a menu of choices, with "recipes," which would allow them to select and customize each design element of a mitten—edgings, cuffs, thumbs, and tops—and combine them with confidence for a completely unique creation. This is that book.

This book is divided into four parts: Designing Your Own Mittens, Components, Techniques, and Patterns. In the Designing Your Own Mittens section, you'll find guidance for all the aesthetic and technical choices that go into creating your own personal mitten patterns. In the Components section, you'll find a gallery of styles for edge treatments, cuffs, thumb constructions, and top shapings. Each example is accompanied by the instructions for its execution. Mix and match to your heart's content to make the mittens of your dreams. In the Techniques chapter, you'll find specific instructions for constructing, embellishing, measuring, and fitting these pieces. All the nuts and bolts you need are here. Need a little inspiration? Just want to follow a traditional mitten recipe? Then head over to the Patterns section, where you'll find twenty complete patterns, just waiting for your personal touches.

I hope you'll enjoy this book, both as a handy reference guide and as a design collection.

Happy knitting; you're in good hands.

How do you like to knit your mittens?

Mittens in this book can be made in any number of ways:

* You can choose to follow a pattern from the Patterns section exactly (see page 66).

* You can customize an existing pattern in the Patterns section (see page 66) by changing one or more of its elements using the Components menu (see page 22) and Techniques section (see page 50).

* You can start from the ground up and invent your own design using a combination of choices from the Components section (see page 22) and adjusting them to fit your yarn and gauge.

FOLLOW A PATTERN

In the Patterns section on page 66, you'll find twenty finished patterns to follow, which offer instructions using a set yarn and gauge. You can knit these designs just as they appear, or substitute the colors and yarns you prefer. The collection includes patterns inspired by traditional knitting styles from around the world, modern interpretations of classic mittens, and brand-new designs to challenge and inspire you. There are mittens to knit from the bottom up, from the top down, and from side to side. The patterns include sizes to fit various hands, but the sizes can be customized easily by adjusting your yarn and gauge (see pages 54–58).

CUSTOMIZE A DESIGN

You can also customize the patterns to suit your fancy. Each pattern includes a breakdown, or "recipe," of the different components used and where you can find them in this book. You can make your own custom creation by swapping out any element for a different one by referring to the Components section (see page 22). The Components section is conceived as a menu of choices. Here you'll find groups of construction options organized by their position on the hand: Edgings, Cuffs, Thumbs, and Tops. Change any of these elements as you wish, using the Mitten Design Worksheet on page 19 as needed to determine or adjust your stitch counts. Make sure to complete gauge swatches so you can determine the proper fit of your finished mittens.

CREATE YOUR OWN

Refer to the Components section to make your own creation! You can pick and choose your favorite elements based on how they look, the way they fit, and the kind of finished mitten you want to make. Just select your components and combine them to make the mittens of your dreams. The instructions for each component are given for worsted-weight yarn, but you can easily change to different yarns and gauges. The Mitten Design Worksheet on page 19 will help you to determine the stitch counts needed for your chosen yarn and gauge. Simply fill in the blanks, and substitute your numbers for those given in the instructions for each component.

You can further reference the Techniques section on page 50 to help make your design decisions and yarn selections. Hand measurements, gauge, wearing ease, and yarn construction are all discussed. Also included is an overview of different construction choices (bottom up, top down, side to side) and why you may want to consider using each. More information on designing your own mittens can be found starting on page 10.

PART 1

DESIGNING YOUR OWN MITTENS

When designing your own mittens, you should first consider the big picture, or the mitten as a whole, and then break it down into its smaller components to get the style and fit you want.

To begin designing, you'll need to make choices about specific elements like gauge, construction direction, and edge treatments. Some decisions can be made as you go or can be left until the end, while others will influence the whole design and need to be made before you start. Some things to consider before you start knitting are gauge, size, and knitting direction. The other decisions can be made as you arrive at each point in the mitten. While you work, make sure to take clear notes about your choices for future reference. They will make knitting the second mitten much easier.

TOP

HAND

THUMB

CUFF

EDGING

Anatomy of a Mitten

Mittens are basically just cylindrical tubes with tapered, closed tops. They typically include a secondary tube, which branches out from the main cylinder, to accommodate the thumb. The cuff area between the lower edge and the base of the thumb may hold the mitten close to the wrist, and/or showcase a stitch or color pattern.

These sections are a mitten's "components," and they're the ingredients you'll modify to create your personal mitten recipes. Each part serves a specific purpose in the whole, and works with the others to cover the hand. Every mitten can be broken down into several parts: edging, cuff, hand, thumb, and top.

The architecture, pattern, and style of these elements determine the finished look. By varying the elements selected, you can create any and every kind of mitten as long as you know the size of the hands you are covering and the gauge of the yarn you'll be using.

GAUGE

All of the samples in the Components section (see page 22) are knit in worsted-weight yarn, with their patterns written for a gauge of 5 stitches and 6 rounds per inch (2.5 cm). If you want to work with a different weight of yarn that will produce a different gauge, you can use the Mitten Design Worksheet on page 19 to calculate new stitch counts.

To determine your gauge, first knit a gauge swatch in your preferred yarn that is big enough to determine how many stitches and rounds are in an inch of your knitted fabric. Since mittens are small, a 4" (10 cm) square should be big enough. This is the time to experiment with

your yarn and needles to create the fabric you like best. Make as many swatches as you like, taking into account how your mittens should fit, feel, and look. For example, do you want your knitting to be firmer or more relaxed (see page 56)? How much ease would you like your mittens to have (see page 54)? Once you feel good about the fabric you've created, wash and block your swatch so you have an accurate starting point for gauge. Then, count how many stitches and rows are in 4" (10 cm) in the center of this fabric (exclude the outer edges of the swatch from this measurement) and divide each number by four to determine your stitches and rounds per inch. Enter these numbers on the worksheet on page 19.

NOTE: *Make sure to mark your swatches in some way to remember which needle size you used. Tie a corresponding number of knots in the cast-on tail, or make the same number of yarnovers in the first row of knitting to help you remember (work a k2tog after each yarnover to maintain the stitch count). Don't measure your swatch in this area, as the gauge may be affected.*

SIZE

To determine the size of your mitten, measure the hand you intend to cover. You need three numbers: the circumference of the hand at its widest point, the length of the hand, and the length of the thumb (see page 53). Enter these numbers as indicated on the worksheet on page 19. Now consider the amount of ease (see page 54). Determine whether you will add or subtract inches (or fractions of inches) from the circumference to create more or less space between the mitten and the hand. Enter any ease adjustment you plan to make on the worksheet.

CONSTRUCTION DIRECTION

Do you want to work from the bottom up, the top down, or from side to side? See page 61 for an overview of your choices. The construction direction will influence the rest of your design decisions and will determine when you have to make them.

LOWER EDGE TREATMENTS

Edge treatments, for the purposes of this book, refer to whatever design element or stitch pattern you use at the very edge of the mitten, below the cuff area. It can be a cast-on/bind-off, a stitch pattern, or an edge component (see page 24) that is worked separately and attached, such as cables or knitted cords. Edges have their own specific stitch counts and/or lengths to which they are worked. Edge treatments may have different stitch counts than your main cylinder and/or cuff. Plan to increase or decrease these as needed to match the number of stitches in your cuff/hand cylinder.

CUFF STYLE

The area between the lower edge treatment and the beginning of the thumb (around the wrist) frequently showcases a pattern or design. You can see examples of this in the Topsy Turvy (see page 126) and Snow Day (see page 106)

designs. Other mittens have a cuff area that is the same measurement and/or stitch pattern as the main hand cylinder, like in the Winter Garden (see page 134) and Lemongrass (see page 118) patterns. If the stitch counts in this area are different from the rest of the mitten (to accommodate stitch or color patterns), make a note of it on the worksheet.

THUMB ARCHITECTURE

The location and construction of your thumb style should be chosen as soon as you have worked your lower edge treatment and/or cuff, because most thumb shaping begins right above the wrist. The single most important factor in the way your mittens fit and feel is the type of thumb you select.

TOP SHAPING

Also keep in mind that different shaping styles result in tops of different lengths. Deeper or shallower top styles commence at different points in the knitting, so be aware of when your chosen shaping starts in order to get the length you need. Unless you are working from the top down, you can wait until you get to the end to decide what kind of mitten top you would like. You can also pick one at the beginning of your project. Top shaping is often specific to different ethnic or geographic knitting styles, and it has a big impact on the style of the mitten. Usually, thumb top shaping that matches that of the mitten top gives the most cohesive look, but you may have reasons to shape your thumb top differently from the top of the mitten.

Design Theory

Establishing a few style guidelines for your design will give you a framework for creating. Applying some simple rules to your work will lend cohesion and intention to your finished product. Here are a few principles to consider as you design.

COLOR

Often, the first thing that we respond to in the look of a mitten is its coloration. Mittens are great accessories to showcase bold or eclectic color choices. Love a color that you wouldn't wear in a larger garment? Mittens are a chance to use it. Consider hand-dyed, color-change, or gradient yarns to make the simplest designs look special. Different knitting techniques can also offer novel ways to incorporate color into your designs. Intarsia, entrelac, and stranded colorwork are all great techniques to try on a small scale for adding color to your mittens. Look at the world around you for color inspiration: Nature (gardens, animals, landscapes), fashion (hot trends, classic looks), and art (old masters, modern mixed media) all can give you ideas for beautiful color combinations in your designs.

TEXTURE

Don't overlook the role of texture in mittens. The simple addition of knit and purl patterns can elevate a plain design. Cables, ribs, and lace are all options that are easily incorporated into mittens. They can be powerfully combined into designs that add up to more than the sum of their parts. Artisanal or novelty yarns can also lend impact to your patterns—here you can showcase special yarns that are too overpowering (or expensive) to use in larger garments. Mittens are perfect for that single ounce of qiviut or the precious few yards of handspun you've been saving.

PROPORTION

Proportion is the scale of a given design element relative to the whole. Keeping different elements in proportion to one another will help your mitten look cohesive. Note the proportions of mittens you like. How are the sizes of the edge, cuff, hand, and top related and balanced? For example, if a mitten has an ornate edge treatment, perhaps the rest of its parts are treated with more restraint. A luxuriously thick cable on the back of the hand might be offset by a smoothly tailored thumb. An area of swirling lace could be juxtaposed against an equal measure of linear ribbing. Make your proportion choices by considering how each part contributes to the whole and which parts you want to emphasize.

REPETITION

Repetition refers to the use of a given element more than once. Echoing a color, pattern, or stitch throughout your mitten strengthens its impact. For example, a pointed top can be repeated by points on the thumbs and the lower edges. Color is also great for repetition. Imagine how placing a row of bright stitches at the lower edge, thumb top, and mitten top might change the look of a neutral mitten. Textured elements are also beautiful when repeated. A simple band of Seed stitch recurring at the cuff, thumb, and top can work magic on a solid-color mitten.

SCANDINAVIAN

FAIR ISLE

GUERNSEY

THRUMMED

Design Inspiration

The best part of knitting your own mittens is that you get to create the exact look, feel, and fit you've always wanted. The combinations are limitless, which is incredibly inspirational, but may seem daunting when you first begin. Fortunately, there have been many knitters throughout the ages who have perfected certain techniques, so you should feel free to pick and choose from their best work to inspire yours. As you begin to plan out your designs, consider exploring some traditional elements that look and function well together.

As you design, think carefully about your yarn choices. The fiber and construction you choose has a big impact on your finished mittens, and some traditional styles are greatly defined by the yarn they employ. You can read more about yarn types and yarn construction on page 58.

SCANDINAVIAN

Norwegian mittens, often referred to as *selbuvotter*, are known for a particular set of hallmarks that are popular throughout Scandinavia. These elements include stranded colorwork in highly contrasting colors, pointed tops and thumbs, and regionally specific pattern motifs. Traditionally, the preferred yarns for Scandinavian mittens have a rounded construction and high twist, which make the patterns stand out in sharp relief. Usually the background of the pattern is in one color (typically a lighter one) and the motifs are in another (usually a darker or brighter color). Scandinavian designs are generally limited to two colors, but sometimes more colors are incorporated, particularly in modern interpretations. A note on technique: *Selbuvotter* are knit without ever changing the orientation of the yarn strands. One strand always passes over the top of the other when changing colors. The strands are never twisted. *Selbuvotter* are typically worked at a medium gauge of approximately 6 stitches to the inch (2.5 cm).

FAIR ISLE

Originating in Scotland, Fair Isle mittens are easily recognizable by their stranded colorwork patterns. The yarn used in Fair Isle–style mittens is traditionally 2-ply Shetland, worked at a fine gauge (typically 6 to 8 stitches to the inch/2.5 cm). Shetland yarns are known for their subtle, heathery colors. Fair Isle–style knitting usually only uses two colors per round, but the two colors used can change as often as every round, creating complicated-looking tonal designs. Fair Isle motifs are also geographically specific and share mathematical properties (they are multiples of one another), which allows them to stack neatly in bands. In Fair Isle knitting, if there are long unused strands, they are tacked down by catching on the wrong side of the work at regular intervals.

GUERNSEY AND ARAN

Typified by the use of single-color yarns (often light or undyed natural shades), mittens from these British Isles get their distinctive patterns from combinations of knit and purl stitches. Guernsey knitting relies on the unique 5-ply, highly-twisted construction of its yarn to create the sharp relief of its stitch definition. Guernsey patterns use knit and purl stitches rather than cables to achieve their delicate look. A firm gauge of 6 or more stitches to the inch (2.5 cm) in sport- or DK-weight yarn also contributes to their dramatic patterning. Aran knits rely on heavier yarns with 3 or more plies and a looser gauge of 4 or 5 stitches to the inch (2.5 cm). The ornate cables of the Aran Islands are, of course, the hallmark of these mittens. Shaping typically calls for rounded tops and thumbs to accommodate the cables, and snug ribbing at the wrist is traditional.

THRUMS AND FULLING

Seen throughout Europe and Canada, mittens designed for optimal warmth are the convention. This extra warmth is designed right into the construction of thrummed and fulled mittens. Thrums are individual lengths of unspun wool roving, knitted along with the yarn at regular intervals. The roving expands into a fluffy fleece lining on the inside of the finished mitten. The gauge of thrummed mittens is large, sometimes only 3 or 4 stitches per inch (2.5 cm). Fulled mittens are worked to a few sizes larger than the hand measurements, then washed and shrunk to fit. Their knitting gauge is relaxed to accommodate this process, say 4 or 5 stitches to the inch (2.5 cm) to begin with, shrinking down to 5 or 6 after fulling. This fabric is less elastic, but wind- and water-resistant. Fulled mittens can be left plain or embellished by color changes and embroidery.

MODERN MITTENS

This category is as inspiring as it is ever-expanding. Advances in our ability to keep warm and new yarn types and blends have allowed knitters to rely less on construction and fiber for basic protection. Now our mittens are free to become works of art and invention, showcasing any and every yarn and technique. There is almost no idea in knitting that can't be translated into a mitten, and I encourage you to experiment with anything that strikes your fancy. Construction, texture, and color are all yours for the taking, and you are free to incorporate any and all of the elements you like best to create mittens that are truly unique.

Mitten Design Worksheet

Fill in the worksheet below to determine the stitch counts you'll need for each component, based on your yarn type and gauge (see pages 56–60). Once you have calculated the appropriate stitch counts, follow the instructions for each component (see page 22), substituting your own stitch counts each time one is indicated.

Direction of construction: _____

Knitting gauge: _____ sts and _____ rounds/rows per inch (2.5 cm) on size _____ needles

MEASUREMENTS

a. Hand circumference: _____ to the nearest ½" (12 mm)

b. Hand length: _____ to the nearest ½" (12 mm)

c. Thumb length: _____ to the nearest ¼" (6 mm)

Multiply the circumference by the number of stitches per inch (2.5 cm): _____

d. Total Hand cylinder sts: _____

Wearing ease: _____ (add or subtract sts per inch, e.g. sts per inch divided by ease required in fractions of an inch, to create more or less space between the mitten and the hand)

Lower edge treatment: _____ (directions found on page _____)

e. Total edge treatment sts: _____ (may be different from Cuff sts)

Cuff style: _____ (directions found on page _____)

Note: To make a snug-fitting cuff, multiply the number on line d by .8 (20% less), then round to the nearest whole number that is a multiple of your cuff stitch pattern.

f. Total Cuff sts: _____

Top style: _____ (directions found on page _____)

g. Decrease _____ sts every round/row

Thumb architecture: _____ (directions found on page _____)

To calculate the total number of thumb stitches you'll need, multiply the number on line d by .33, then round to the nearest whole number (actual thumb stitch count may be even or odd, depending on component chosen).

h. Total Thumb sts: _____

i. Cast-on sts: _____ (from line e)

Here's an example of what the worksheet looks like in action. Let's assume you wanted to combine the following mitten components:

Edge: Knitted Picot Hem (see page 29)
Cuff: Horizontal Rib (see page 34)
Thumb: Western Gusset (see page 43)
Top: Spoke (see page 49)

Let's further assume that you chose to work from the bottom up, you've taken your hand measurements, and you've decided to use DK-weight yarn with a gauge of 6 stitches and 7 rounds per inch (2.5 cm):

Direction of construction: _____*bottom-up*_____

Knitting gauge: ___*6*___ sts and ___*7*___ rounds/rows per inch (2.5 cm) on size ___*4*___ needles

MEASUREMENTS

a. Hand circumference: ___*8″*___ to the nearest ½" (12 mm)

b. Hand length: ___*7″*___ to the nearest ½" (12 mm)

c. Thumb length: ___*2½″*___ to the nearest ¼" (6 mm)

Multiply the circumference by the number of stitches per inch (2.5 cm): ___*8 × 6 = 48 sts*___

d. Total Hand cylinder sts: ___*48*___

Wearing ease: ___*0*___ (add or subtract sts per inch, e.g. sts per inch divided by ease required in fractions of an inch, to create more or less space between the mitten and the hand)

Lower edge treatment: _____*Knitted Picot Hem*_____ (directions found on page ___*29*___)

e. Total edge treatment sts: ___*38*___ (may be different from Cuff sts)

Cuff style: _____*Horizontal Rib*_____ (directions found on page ___*34*___)

f. Total Cuff sts: ___*38*___

Top style: _____*Spoke*_____ (directions found on page ___*49*___)

g. Decrease ___*8*___ sts every round/row

Thumb architecture: _____*Western Gusset*_____ (directions found on page ___*43*___)

h. Total Thumb sts: ___*16*___

i. Cast-on sts: ___*38*___ (from line e)

You now have your own personal knitting pattern, which would go like this:

MITTENS

With MC, CO 38 sts. Join for working in the rnd, being careful not to twist sts; pm for beginning of rnd.

HEM

Work Knitted Picot Hem (see page 29), substituting your st count (38).

CUFF

Work in Horizontal Rib until piece measures 3" (7.5 cm) from Picot Edge, or to desired Cuff length.

Knit 1 rnd, increasing 10 sts evenly to end—48 sts. Change to Hand st pattern.

SHAPE THUMB GUSSET

Work Western Gusset Thumb (see page 43), substituting your Thumb st count (15).

HAND

Work even until piece measures 5" (12.5 cm) from end of Cuff, or approximately 2" (5 cm) less than desired Hand length.

SHAPE MITTEN TOP

Work Spoke Top (see page 49), substituting your st count (48, or 8 sts per Spoke segment).

THUMB

Transfer Thumb Gusset sts to needles; rejoin yarn.

Pick up and knit 1 st at base of Thumb—16 sts.

Join for working in the rnd; pm for beginning of rnd.

Work even until Thumb measures 2" (5 cm), or to ½" (12 mm) less than desired Thumb length.

Work Thumb decreases as desired (to match Top, work four Spoke segments with 4 sts each).

FINISHING

Weave in ends. Block Mittens.

Make photocopies of the Mitten Design Worksheet so you can try as many different combinations as you want. Remember, keep all your notes from the first mitten so you can use them for the second one.

PART 2

COMPONENTS

Welcome to the components section. This is the menu from which you can choose all the elements of your own personal mitten design. Some of these shapes can be seen in different iterations in the Patterns section (see page 66), while others are only shown here.

Each sample photo depicts a single-color version of part of a mitten. The samples are all knit from worsted-weight wool yarn at a gauge of 5 stitches and 6 rounds to the inch (2.5 cm). To change the gauge of a given component, refer to the Mitten Design Worksheet on page 19.

The direction of knitting is noted for each sample, as well as its reversibility (if it can be worked from either the bottom up or from the top down). When a given component can be worked in reverse, directions for doing so are included. Not sure which component to choose? You can easily make a "trial run" version in worsted-weight yarn to see how its construction works. Just follow the accompanying directions for each piece as written.

Let your imagination be your guide, and most important, enjoy the process of designing your own mittens!

NOTE: *"Reversible" refers to top down vs. bottom up direction.*

Edges

This section contains a selection of treatments for the lower edges of your mittens. Instructions are given for top down and/or bottom up constructions, while some edges are "reversible" and can be worked in either direction. Edges look great when combined with other cuff components, or can be used on their own as replacements for cuffs.

Don't underestimate the power of lower edge treatments in your finished mitten design. If you think of your mitten as artwork, its edges are the frame around it. Lower edge treatments look great when repeated at the tops and thumbs of fingerless mitts, too. You can also change the color or stitch pattern of an edge treatment to multiply your choices.

CORDED EDGE,
PAGE 25

LATVIAN
BRAID,
PAGE 26

PICOT
CAST-ON,
PAGE 26

LOOPED FRINGE
CAST-ON,
PAGE 27

BOBBLED EDGE,
PAGE 27

CHANNEL ISLAND
CAST-ON,
PAGE 28

RUFFLED
EDGE,
PAGE 29

KNITTED
PICOT HEM,
PAGE 29

Worked from the bottom up
The Knitted Cord is worked separately, then the mitten is picked up and knit along one edge of it.

With dpn, CO 5 sts.

Next Row (RS): K5. Do not turn. *Slide sts to opposite end of needle, k5; repeat from * until Cord measures 20" (51 cm).

Break yarn, leaving a long tail. Thread tail through all sts, pull tight, pull tail to inside of Cord, and trim. Pull CO tail to inside of Cord and trim. Fold Cord in half to locate center. Beginning 29 rows from center, working through one column of sts and picking up at a rate of 3 sts for every 4 rows, pick up and knit 44 sts (22 sts before center and 22 sts after center). Join for working in the rnd, being careful not to twist sts; pm for beginning of rnd. Tie Cord ends into a bow.

Worked from the top down
The Knitted Cord is worked adjacent to live stitches, attaching to and binding off each st at the same time.

Work Cord as at left to a length of 6" (15 cm) (length of unattached Cord).

Transfer 5 Cord sts to left needle, to right of Mitten sts.

Next Row (RS): *[K4 Cord sts, ssk (1 Cord st with next Mitten st), transfer 5 sts to left needle] 3 times, k5, transfer 5 sts to left needle; repeat from * until all Mitten sts have been worked—5 Cord sts remain.

Work Cord sts alone as above to a length of 6" (15 cm).

Break yarn, leaving a long tail. Thread tail through all sts, pull tight, pull tail to inside of Cord, and trim. Pull CO tail to inside of Cord and trim. Tie Cord ends into a bow.

To work a plain Corded Edge from either direction, omit the extra length on each knitted Cord end and graft the ends with matching yarn.

LATVIAN BRAID (REVERSIBLE)

PICOT CAST-ON (REVERSIBLE)

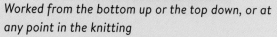

Worked from the bottom up or the top down, or at any point in the knitting

Rnd 1: *K1 with MC, k1 with CC; repeat from * to end.

Rnd 2: Move both strands to front of work. *P1 with MC, p1 with CC, bringing each strand up from **under** prior strand with every st ; repeat from * to end (strands will twist around each other in this rnd, and untwist in the next one).

Rnd 3: *P1 with MC, p1 with CC, crossing each strand **over** prior strand with every st; repeat from * to end.

These 3 rnds comprise the braid, and can be worked across any even number of sts, at any location in the knitting.

Worked from the bottom up
As a cast-on

Using Cable CO (see *Special Techniques*, page 154), *CO 8 sts, BO 3 sts, transfer 1 st from right needle to left needle; repeat from * until 45 sts are CO.

Note: *You can adjust the amount of space between picots by casting on more or fewer sts between them (in the sample there are 5). You can adjust the size of the picots by casting on and then binding off more or fewer sts for each (in the sample there are 3).*

Worked from the top down
As a bind-off

Beginning with 45 sts, BO 5 sts, *transfer 1 st from right needle to left needle, Cable CO 3 sts, BO 8 sts; repeat from * until 1 st remains on right needle (no sts on left needle), transfer 1 st from right needle to left needle, CO 3 sts, BO all sts. Break yarn. Thread tail through last st, pull tight, and fasten off to WS.

LOOPED FRINGE CAST-ON

BOBBLED EDGE (REVERSIBLE)

Worked from the bottom up
Leaving a tail of approximately 3 yards (2.7 m), make a slipknot and place it on the needle. Hold the yarn as for Long-Tail CO (see *Special Techniques*, page 154), making sure the yarn strand coming from the skein goes over your index finger, and the tail strand goes over your thumb.

A. Pass the needle under the front strand of the loop formed by the thumb from left to right (just as for Long-Tail CO).

B. Pass the needle from right to left over both strands formed by the index finger. The loop around your index finger will be the loop of fringe.

C. Leaving the loop around your index finger, pass both strands through the thumb loop (the new st on the needle will have 2 strands).

D. Use your thumb and forefinger to tighten the thumb loop around the new double st; remove your index finger from the loop. Return thumb and index finger to original positions.

Repeat steps A–D to CO as many sts as needed. The tightness of the new double st and the length of the loop can be adjusted by gently pulling on one strand or the other before making the next st. Be sure not to pull too tightly or you will undo the loop. When working the first row after the CO, work each double st as a single st.

Worked from the bottom up
As a cast-on
Using Cable CO (see *Special Techniques*, page 154), *CO 6 sts. K1-f/b/f/b, [transfer 4 sts to left needle, k4] 3 times, pass second, third, and fourth sts on right needle over first. Slip 1 st to right needle and pass bobble st over it. Pull working strand to snug bobble and close gap. Transfer st to left needle—5 sts CO. Repeat from * until 45 sts are CO. On following rnd, knit tbl of each bobble st.

Worked from the top down
As a bind-off
*BO 6 sts. Transfer 1 st from right needle to left needle. K1-f/b/f/b, [transfer 4 sts to left needle, k4] 3 times, pass second, third, and fourth sts on right needle over first. Slip 1 st to right needle and pass bobble st over it. Pull working strand to snug bobble and close gap. Transfer st to left needle—7 sts BO. Repeat from * until all sts are BO.

Break yarn. Thread tail through last st, pull tight, and fasten off to WS.

Note: *Keep st and working yarn loose, especially when knitting into front and back of st, to make it easier to work bobbles.*

Worked from the bottom up

Pull out approximately 3 yards (2.7 m) of yarn from the skein and fold it in thirds. Holding all 3 strands as one, make a slipknot approximately 6" (15 cm) away from the cut end. Place slipknot on needle (this triple strand does not count as a st; you'll remove it later). With the needle in your right hand, separate the skein strand and the doubled "tail" strand (the loop). Wrap the doubled "tail" strand counter-clockwise twice around the left thumb (opposite of the direction of wrap of Long-Tail CO [see *Special Techniques*, page 154]). Hold the single strand over the index finger (as for Long-Tail CO).

A. Scoop the needle under the single index finger strand from right to left, creating a yo on the needle. Hold it in place with your right index finger for the next step.

B. Insert the needle up through both double-strand wraps on the thumb, then over the top of the single index strand, then down through the thumb loops, creating a new single-strand st on the needle. Drop the loops off the thumb and pull the double-strand end to tighten it into a knot beneath the new st.

C. Reset the strands for the next 2 sts as before, wrapping the double strand counter-clockwise twice around the thumb.

Repeat steps A–C to create 44 sts, or as many sets of 2 as needed. When joining for working in the rnd, drop the original 3-strand slipknot from the needle.

Note: *Traditionally, this CO is followed by 1x1 Rib, with the knit sts falling over the double-strand "bumps" of the CO, and the purls falling over the single-strand "divots."*

RUFFLED EDGE (REVERSIBLE)

KNITTED PICOT HEM (REVERSIBLE)

Worked from the bottom up
Decreased ruffle
CO 132 sts (3 times the desired number of sts).
Join for working in the rnd, being careful not to
twist sts; pm for beginning of rnd. Knit 6 rnds.

Next Rnd: *S2kp2; repeat from * to end—44 sts
remain.

Worked from the top down
Increased ruffle
With 44 sts, work Hand and Cuff to desired
length.

Increase Rnd: *K1-f/b/f; repeat from * to
end—132 sts. Knit 6 rnds. Loosely BO all sts.

Worked from the bottom up
As a cast-on
CO 44 sts. Join for working in the rnd, being
careful not to twist sts; pm for beginning of rnd.
Knit 6 rnds.

Picot Rnd: *K2tog, yo; repeat from * to end. Knit
5 rnds. Fold hem to WS along Picot Rnd.

Next Rnd: *Insert left needle into first CO st and
k2tog (CO st and next st on needle); repeat from
* for each CO st—44 sts remain.

Worked from the top down
As a bind-off
Work Cuff to 6 rnds from desired length. Knit
6 rnds.

Picot Rnd: *K2tog, yo; repeat from * to end. Knit
5 rnds. Fold hem to WS along Picot Rnd.

Next Rnd: Insert left needle into st 12 rnds
directly below st on left needle and k2tog (st
from 12 rnds below and next st on needle), *insert
left needle into st 12 rnds directly below st on left
needle and k2tog (st from 12 rnds below and next
st on needle), pass second st on right needle over
first to BO 1 st; repeat from * until all sts are BO.

Break yarn. Thread tail through last st, pull tight,
and fasten off to WS.

Note for Knitted Picot Hem: *To practice working
this edge, change yarn colors after the CO rnd (or
first rnd of hem, for BO). This way, when you join
the hem, you'll be pulling the new color through
the old one, making it easier to see.*

Cuffs

Here is a collection of cuff styles for your mittens. Long and short, simple and fancy, flared and straight: These are intended to spark your creativity and inspire your designs. Cuffs are an ideal place to showcase special yarns, colors, or stitch techniques, so let your imagination run free when you envision them.

SIDELONG
CABLE,
PAGE 31

DELLA ROBBIA
CABLE,
PAGE 32

FRENCH CUFF,
PAGE 33

HORIZONTAL
RIB,
PAGE 34

CORRUGATED
RIB,
PAGE 34

DRAWSTRING,
PAGE 35

CABLED
GAUNTLET,
PAGE 36

LEAVES CUFF,
PAGE 37

SIDELONG CABLE

Worked back and forth in rows from the bottom up, then joined in the rnd

Using Provisional CO (see *Special Techniques*, page 155), CO 13 sts.

Note: *First row of chart is a WS row.* Working back and forth in rows, work Rows 1–8 of chart until piece measures 8" (20.5 cm), ending with Row 8.

Unpick Provisional CO and place sts onto a spare needle. With RS together and using Three-Needle BO (see *Special Techniques*, page 155), join ends. Break yarn. Thread tail through last st, pull tight, and fasten off to WS.

With RS facing, pick up and knit 44 sts along lower edge of piece. Join for working in the rnd; pm for beginning of rnd. Knit 6 rnds.

Turning Rnd: Purl. Knit 5 rnds. Fold hem to WS along Turning Rnd.

Next Rnd: Insert left needle into st 12 rnds directly below st on left needle and k2tog (st from 12 rnds below and next st on needle),

*insert left needle into st 12 rnds directly below st on left needle and k2tog (st from 12 rnds below and next st on needle), pass second st on right needle over first to BO 1 st; repeat from * until all sts are BO.

Break yarn. Thread tail through last st, pull tight, and fasten off to WS. With RS facing, pick up and knit 44 sts along top edge of piece.

Continue Mitten as desired.

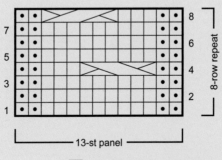

Knit on RS, purl on WS.

• Purl on RS, knit on WS.

Slip 3 sts to cn, hold to back, k3, k3 from cn.

Slip 3 sts to cn, hold to front, k3, k3 from cn.

Worked back and forth in rows from the bottom up, then joined in the rnd

Using Provisional CO (see *Special Techniques*, page 155), CO 15 sts.

Note: *First row of chart is a WS row.* Working back and forth in rows, work Rows 1–20 of chart 4 times. Unpick Provisional CO and place sts onto a spare needle. With RS together and using Three-Needle BO (see *Special Techniques*, page 155), join ends.

Break yarn. Thread tail through last st, pull tight, and fasten off to WS.

With RS facing, pick up and knit 54 sts along lower edge of cable. Join for working in the rnd; pm for beginning of rnd. Work 2 rnds of 1x1 Rib. BO using Tubular BO (see *Special Techniques*, page 155), or in pattern using your preferred BO.

With RS facing, pick up and knit 44 sts along upper edge of cable. Join for working in the rnd; pm for beginning of rnd. Work 6 rnds of 1x1 Rib.

Continue Mitten as desired.

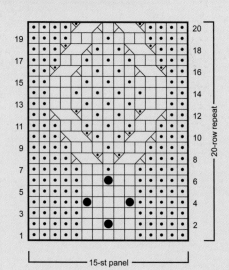

☐	Knit on RS, purl on WS.
⊡	Purl on RS, knit on WS.
●	K1-f/b/f/b/f, turn; p5, turn; k5, turn; p5, turn; k5, pass second, third, fourth, and fifth sts over first.
⟋	Slip 1 st to cn, hold to back, k2, p1 from cn.
⟍	Slip 2 sts to cn, hold to front, p1, k2 from cn.

Worked back and forth in rows from the bottom up, then joined in the rnd
Using MC and Tubular CO (see *Special Techniques*, page 155) or CO of your choice, CO 56 sts.

Next Row (RS): *K1, p1; repeat from * to end.

Next Row (WS): *P1, k1; repeat from * to end.
Repeat last 2 rows until piece measures 2¼"
(5.5 cm), ending with a RS row. BO 6 sts at beg of next 2 rows—44 sts remain.
Join for working in the rnd; pm for beginning of rnd.

Continue Mitten as desired.

Knot (make 2 for each cuff)
With CC and dpn, CO 5 sts.

Next Row (RS): K5. Do not turn. *Slide sts to opposite end of needle, k5; repeat from * until Cord measures 2½" (6 cm).
Break yarn, leaving a long tail. Thread tail through all sts, pull tight, and fasten off.

Tie Cord into an overhand knot. Tie CO and BO tails into a square knot. Sew one Knot to each side of Cuff (like cufflinks) at desired location, sewing through both layers of cuff to secure.

HORIZONTAL RIB

CORRUGATED RIB

Worked in rnds from the bottom up
CO 44 sts. Join for working in the rnd, being careful not to twist sts; pm for beginning of rnd. *Knit 4 rnds. Purl 3 rnds. Repeat from * twice.

Continue Mitten as desired.

Worked in rnds from the bottom up
Using MC and Tubular CO (see *Special Techniques*, page 155) or CO of your choice, CO 44 sts. Join for working in the rnd, being careful not to twist sts; pm for beginning of rnd. Work 1 rnd of 2x2 Rib. Join CC.

Next Rnd: *K2 with MC, k2 with CC; repeat from * to end.

Next Rnd: *K2 with MC, p2 with CC; repeat from * to end. Repeat last rnd 6 times.

Break CC. Continue Mitten as desired.

Worked in rnds from the bottom up
Using MC and Tubular CO (see *Special Techniques*, page 155) or CO of your choice, CO 50 sts. Join for working in the rnd, being careful not to twist sts; pm for beginning of rnd. Work 2 rnds of 1x1 Rib. Knit 6 rnds.

Eyelet Rnd: *K3, k2tog, yo; repeat from * to end. Knit 5 rnds. Repeat Eyelet Rnd.

Continue Mitten as desired.

Knitted Cords
With CC1 and dpn, CO 4 sts.

Next Row (RS): K4. Do not turn. *Slide sts to opposite end of needle, k4; repeat from * until Cord measures 12" (30.5 cm).

Break yarn, leaving a long tail. Thread tail through all sts, pull tight, pull tail to inside of Cord, and trim.

Pull CO tail to inside of Cord and trim.

Make second Cord with CC2. Weave Cords through Eyelets and tie into square knots.

Worked in rnds from the bottom up
CO 88 sts. Join for working in the rnd, being careful not to twist sts; pm for beginning of rnd. Work Rnds 1–27 of chart—40 sts remain.

Increase Rnd: P2, M1, *k2, p3, k2, p3, M1; repeat from * to last 8 sts, k2, p3, k2, p1—44 sts.

Continue Mitten as desired.

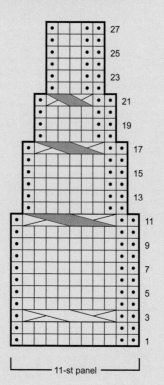

Knit

Purl

Slip 2 sts to cn, hold to front, k2tog, k2tog from cn—2 sts decreased.

Slip 3 sts to cn, hold to front, k1, k2tog, (k2tog, k1) from cn—2 sts decreased.

Slip 4 sts to cn, hold to front, k2tog, k2, (k2, k2tog) from cn—2 sts decreased.

Slip 4 sts to cn, hold to front, k4, k4 from cn.

⌐ 11-st panel ⌐

Worked back and forth in rows from the bottom up, then joined in the rnd
Using Provisional CO (see *Special Techniques*, page 155), CO 6 sts. Working back and forth in rows, work Rows 1–14 of chart 6 times.

Unpick Provisional CO and place sts onto a spare needle. With RS together and using Three-Needle BO (see *Special Techniques*, page 155), join ends.

Break yarn. Thread tail through last st, pull tight, and fasten off to WS.

With RS facing, pick up and knit 44 sts along top (garter) edge. Join for working in the rnd; pm for beginning of rnd. Work 12 rnds of 2x2 Rib.

Continue Mitten as desired.

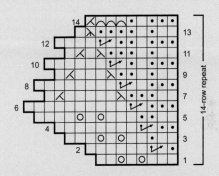

14-row repeat

☐ Knit on RS, purl on WS.
• Purl on RS, knit on WS.
O Yo
∟ K1-f/b on WS.

◩ K2tog on RS, p2tog on WS.
◪ Ssk
◪ Sk2p
◠ BO

Thumbs

The thumb style you choose will have a big impact on the finished look and feel of your mittens. The following pages showcase a selection of choices to get you started, each with its own distinctive architecture and advantages. Some can be worked top down or bottom up, some are interchangeable from left to right mittens, and some are specific to the left or right mitten. All the instructions here are given for bottom up, but you can work them in reverse by changing increases to decreases if you wish.

Different mitten thumb styles all have one thing in common: Extra knitted fabric is created to accommodate the digit, branching off from the main hand cylinder of knitting. It's amazing how many ways there are to do this. Some take one or more stitches from the hand to make the thumb, and fill in new hand stitches (either increased or cast on) to replace them. Others work the other way around, leaving the hand cylinder stitches intact, and relying completely on increased or cast-on stitches to make the thumb. Still others do a little of each, with some of the thumb stitches borrowed from the hand, and others cast on or increased as well. Thumbs are also placed in slightly different locations on the mitten in different architectures: on the side of the hand, off-center on the palm, or growing up out of the inner wrist.

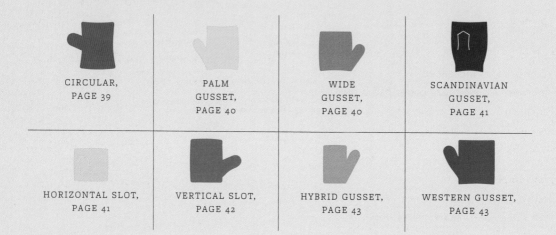

| CIRCULAR, PAGE 39 | PALM GUSSET, PAGE 40 | WIDE GUSSET, PAGE 40 | SCANDINAVIAN GUSSET, PAGE 41 |
| HORIZONTAL SLOT, PAGE 41 | VERTICAL SLOT, PAGE 42 | HYBRID GUSSET, PAGE 43 | WESTERN GUSSET, PAGE 43 |

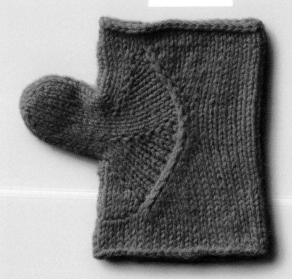

Worked separately first, then mitten is knit and attached to it simultaneously
Left/right interchangeable
Using Judy's Magic CO (see *Special Techniques*, page 154), CO 3 sts onto each of 2 needles—6 sts. Knit 1 rnd.

Increase Rnd 1: *K1, M1R, knit to last st of needle, M1L, k1; repeat from * once more—4 sts increased.
Repeat Increase Rnd 1 every other rnd twice—18 sts. Knit 13 rnds, or to desired Thumb length.

Next Rnd: *K3, pm; repeat from * to end.

Increase Rnd 2: *Knit to marker, M1, sm; repeat from * to end—6 sts increased.
Repeat Increase Rnd 2 every other rnd 5 times—54 sts. Knit 1 rnd. Set aside, leaving sts on needles. Work Edge and/or Cuff treatment(s) of choice, ending with 44 Hand sts.

Join Thumb to Hand

With RS together and using Three-Needle BO (see *Special Techniques*, page 155), join first 10 sts of each piece—44 Thumb sts and 34 Hand sts remain.

Working back and forth in rows, join remaining Thumb sts to Hand as follows:

Next Row (RS): Slip 1, knit to last 3 Hand sts, ssk, ssk (last Hand st and 1 Thumb st), turn—2 sts decreased.
Next Row (WS): Slip 1, purl to last 3 hand sts, p2tog, p2tog (last Hand st and 1 Thumb st), turn—2 sts decreased.
Repeat last 2 rows 6 times—30 Thumb sts and 20 Hand sts remain.

Next Row (RS): Slip 1, knit to last Hand st, ssk (last Hand st and 1 Thumb st), turn—1 st decreased.
Next Row (WS): Slip 1, purl to last Hand st, p2tog (last Hand st and 1 Thumb st), turn—1 st decreased.
Repeat last 2 rows twice—24 Thumb sts and 20 Hand sts remain.

Next Row (RS): Slip 1, knit to last Hand st, M1L, ssk (last Hand st and 1 Thumb st), turn.
Next Row (WS): Slip 1, purl to last Hand st, M1PR, p2tog (last Hand st and 1 Thumb st), turn.
Repeat last 2 rows 5 times—12 Thumb sts and 32 Hand sts remain; 44 sts total. Work in the rnd across all 44 sts.

Complete Mitten as desired.

PALM GUSSET

WIDE GUSSET

Worked together with hand.
Left/right interchangeable
Work Edging and/or Cuff of choice, ending with 44 sts.

Next Rnd: K15, pm, k14, pm, k15.

Increase Rnd: Knit to marker, M1R, sm, k14, sm, M1L, knit to end—2 Hand sts increased outside markers.

Repeat Increase Rnd every other rnd 6 times—14 Thumb sts and 44 Hand sts. Knit 1 rnd.

Next Rnd: Knit to marker, remove marker, place 14 Thumb Gusset sts on waste yarn, remove marker, knit to end—44 Hand sts remain.

Complete Mitten as desired.

Transfer Thumb Gusset sts to needles; rejoin yarn. Join for working in the rnd; pm for beginning of rnd. Work 12 rnds, or to desired Thumb length. Shape Thumb Top as desired.

Worked together with hand
Left/right interchangeable
Work Edging and/or Cuff of choice, ending with 44 sts.

Next Rnd: K19, pm, k6, pm, knit to end.

Increase Rnd: Knit to marker, sm, M1R, knit to marker, M1L, sm, knit to end—2 sts increased between markers.

Repeat Increase Rnd every third rnd twice—12 Thumb Gusset sts and 38 Hand sts. Knit 2 rnds.

Next Rnd: Knit to marker, remove marker, place 12 Thumb Gusset sts on waste yarn, remove marker, CO 4 sts, knit to end—42 sts remain.

Complete Mitten as desired.

Transfer Thumb Gusset sts to needles; rejoin yarn. Pick up and knit 4 sts along CO edge at gap—16 sts. Join for working in the rnd; pm for beginning of rnd. Work 12 rnds, or to desired Thumb length. Shape Thumb Top as desired.

SCANDINAVIAN GUSSET

HORIZONTAL SLOT

Worked together with hand
Not left/right interchangeable
Work Edging and/or Cuff of choice, ending with 37 sts. Beginning of rnd is at the inside of hand, beneath the index finger.

Left Mitten Only / Next Rnd: K27, pm, k2, pm, knit to end.
Right Mitten Only / Next Rnd: K8, pm, k2, pm, knit to end.

Both Mittens
Increase Rnd: Knit to marker, sm, k1-f/b, knit to 1 st before marker, k1-f/b, sm, knit to end—2 sts increased between markers.
Repeat Increase Rnd every third rnd twice—8 Thumb Gusset sts and 35 Hand sts. Knit 2 rnds.

Next Rnd: Knit to marker, remove marker, k1, place 7 Thumb Gusset sts on waste yarn, remove marker, CO 7 sts, knit to end—43 sts.

Complete Mitten as desired.
Transfer 7 Thumb Gusset sts to needles; rejoin yarn. Pick up and knit 7 sts along CO edge at gap—14 sts. Join for working in the rnd; pm for beginning of rnd. Work 12 rnds, or to desired Thumb length. Shape Thumb Top as desired.

Worked from held palm sts
Not left/right interchangeable
Work Edging and/or Cuff of choice, ending with 44 sts. Beginning of rnd is at the outside of hand, beneath the little finger.

Left Mitten Only / Next Rnd: K12, k7 with waste yarn, transfer 7 waste yarn sts to left needle, knit to end.

Right Mitten Only / Next Rnd: K25, k7 with waste yarn, transfer 7 waste yarn sts to left needle, knit to end.

Both Mittens
Complete Mitten as desired.

Unpick waste yarn sts one at a time, placing sts onto 2 needles. Rejoin yarn.

Next Rnd: K7 from lower needle, M1 at gap, k7 from upper needle, M1 at gap—16 sts. Work 16 rnds, or to desired Thumb length. Shape Thumb Top as desired.

Worked from opening made in side of hand
Left/right interchangeable
Work Edging and/or Cuff of choice, ending with 44 sts.

Next Row (RS): K44, turn.

Next Row (WS): P44, turn.

Repeat last 2 rows until Slot Opening measures 2" (5 cm), or approximately 13 rows, ending with a RS row. Rejoin for working in the rnd; pm for beginning of rnd. Complete Mitten as desired.

Rejoin yarn at top of Slot. With RS facing, pick up and knit 24 sts around opening. Join for working in the rnd; pm for beginning of rnd.

Rnd 1: Knit.

Rnd 2: K10, ssk, k2tog, k10—22 sts remain.

Rnd 3: Knit.

Rnd 4: K9, ssk, k2tog, k9—20 sts remain.

Rnd 5: Knit.

Rnd 6: K8, ssk, k2tog, k8—18 sts remain.

Rnd 7: Knit.

Rnd 8: K7, ssk, k2tog, k7—16 sts remain.

Knit 12 rnds, or to desired Thumb length. Shape Thumb Top as desired.

HYBRID GUSSET

WESTERN GUSSET

Worked together with hand
Left/right interchangeable
Work Edging and/or Cuff of choice, ending with 45 sts.

Next Rnd: K22, pm, k1, pm, k22.

Increase Rnd: K22, sm, yo, knit to marker, yo, sm, knit to end—2 sts increased.

Repeat Increase Rnd every third rnd 5 times—13 Thumb Gusset sts and 44 Hand sts. Knit 2 rnds.

Next Rnd: Knit to marker, remove marker, place 13 Thumb Gusset sts on waste yarn, remove marker, CO 3 sts, knit to end—47 sts remain.

Complete Mitten as desired.

Transfer Thumb Gusset sts to needles; rejoin yarn. Pick up and knit 3 sts along CO edge at gap—16 sts. Join for working in the rnd; pm for beginning of rnd. Work 12 rnds, or to desired Thumb length. Shape Thumb Top as desired.

Worked together with hand
Left/right interchangeable
Work Edging and/or Cuff of choice, ending with 45 sts.

Next Rnd: K22, pm, k1, pm, k22.

Increase Rnd: Knit to marker, sm, M1R, knit to marker, M1L, sm, knit to end—2 sts increased.

Repeat Increase Rnd every third rnd 6 times—15 Thumb Gusset sts and 44 Hand sts. Knit 2 rnds.

Next Rnd: Knit to marker, remove marker, place 15 Thumb Gusset sts on waste yarn, remove marker, CO 1 st, knit to end—45 sts remain.

Complete Mitten as desired. Transfer Thumb Gusset sts to needles; rejoin yarn. Join for working in the rnd; pm for beginning of rnd. Work 12 rnds, or to desired Thumb length. Shape Thumb Top as desired.

Tops

The top of your mitten does more than cover your fingers; it also finishes and highlights the style of the hand cylinder. Choose your top shaping based on your fitting requirements, the construction that best accommodates your stitch or color motifs, or both. Think about how much "wiggle room" you'd like, as well as the look of your mitten's finished silhouette. Some tops decrease at a faster rate for a shallower fit, or decrease more slowly for a deeper one. Traditional and other style influences will also affect your choices. Most styles can be worked from the top down with increases instead of decreases, and almost all are reversible from left to right. Mitten top decreases are usually made at either regular intervals around the circumference of the hand cylinder for a round tubular top, or at static points on its sides for a flat one. You'll find a little of everything in this section, so it's a great opportunity to try something new.

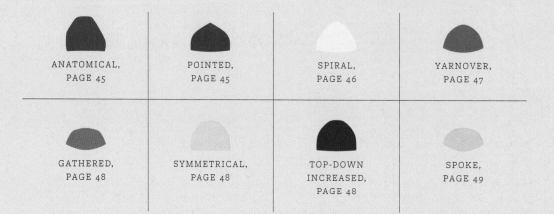

ANATOMICAL,
PAGE 45

POINTED,
PAGE 45

SPIRAL,
PAGE 46

YARNOVER,
PAGE 47

GATHERED,
PAGE 48

SYMMETRICAL,
PAGE 48

TOP-DOWN
INCREASED,
PAGE 48

SPOKE,
PAGE 49

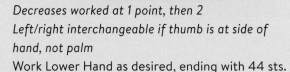

Decreases worked at 1 point, then 2
Left/right interchangeable if thumb is at side of
hand, not palm
Work Lower Hand as desired, ending with 44 sts.

Next Rnd: K22, pm, k22.

Decrease Rnd 1: K1, ssk, knit to last 3 sts, k2tog, k1—2 sts decreased.

Repeat Decrease Rnd 1 every other rnd once—40 sts remain. Work 1 rnd even.

Decrease Rnd 2: *K1, ssk, knit to 3 sts before marker, k2tog, k1, sm; repeat from * once—4 sts decreased.

Repeat Decrease Rnd 2 every other rnd 4 times—20 sts remain. Place 10 sts onto each of 2 needles. Using Kitchener st (see *Special Techniques*, page 154), graft Top.

Decreases worked at 2 points
Left/right interchangeable
Work Lower Hand as desired, ending with 44 sts.

Next Rnd: K22, pm, k22. **Note:** *Decreases are worked every round.*

Decrease Rnd: *K1, ssk, knit to 2 sts before marker, k2tog; repeat from * once—4 sts decreased.

Repeat Decrease Rnd every rnd 8 times— 8 sts remain.

Next Rnd: [K1, s2kp2] twice—4 sts remain.

Break yarn, leaving a long tail. Thread tail onto a tapestry needle.

To close Top, remove needles from last 4 sts. Use the tip of the tapestry needle or a crochet hook to pull left side st through right side st and thread tail through left side st. Pull center back st through center front st and thread tail through center back st. Fasten off to WS.

Decreases worked at 5 points incrementally
Left/right interchangeable

Work Lower Hand as desired, ending with 45 sts.

Rnd 1: *K7, k2tog; repeat from * to end—40 sts remain.

Rnd 2: Knit.

Rnd 3: *K6, k2tog; repeat from * to end—35 sts remain.

Rnd 4: Knit.

Rnd 5: *K5, k2tog; repeat from * to end—30 sts remain.

Rnd 6: Knit.

Rnd 7: *K4, k2tog; repeat from * to end—25 sts remain.

Rnd 8: Knit.

Rnd 9: *K3, k2tog; repeat from * to end—20 sts remain.

Rnd 10: Knit.

Rnd 11: *K2, k2tog; repeat from * to end—15 sts remain.

Rnd 12: Knit.

Rnd 13: *K1, k2tog; repeat from * to end—10 sts remain.

Rnd 14: Knit.

Rnd 15: *K2tog; repeat from * to end—5 sts remain.

Break yarn, leaving a long tail. Thread tail through remaining sts, pull tight, and fasten off to WS.

Decreases worked at 5 points incrementally
Left/right interchangeable
Work Lower Hand as desired, ending with
45 sts.

Rnd 1: *K5, k2tog, yo, k2tog; repeat from * to
end—40 sts remain.

Rnd 2: Knit.

Rnd 3: *K4, k2tog, yo, k2tog; repeat from * to
end—35 sts remain.

Rnd 4: Knit.

Rnd 5: *K3, k2tog, yo, k2tog; repeat from * to
end—30 sts remain.

Rnd 6: Knit.

Rnd 7: *K2, k2tog, yo, k2tog; repeat from * to
end—25 sts remain.

Rnd 8: Knit.

Rnd 9: *K1, k2tog, yo, k2tog; repeat from * to
end—20 sts remain.

Rnd 10: Knit.

Rnd 11: *K2tog, yo, k2tog; repeat from * to
end—15 sts remain.

Rnd 12: Knit.

Rnd 13: *Sk2p; repeat from * to end—5 sts
remain.

Break yarn, leaving a long tail. Thread tail
through remaining sts, pull tight, and fasten
off to WS.

Decreases worked evenly around
Left/right interchangeable
Work Lower Hand as desired, ending with
44 sts.

Rnd 1: [K2tog] 22 times—22 sts remain.
Rnd 2: Knit.
Rnd 3: [K2tog] 11 times—11 sts remain.
Rnd 4: Knit.
Break yarn, leaving a long tail. Thread tail
through remaining sts, pull tight, and fasten off
to WS.

SYMMETRICAL

Decreases worked at 2 points
Left/right interchangeable
Work Lower Hand as desired, ending with
44 sts.

Next Rnd: K22, pm, k22.
Decrease Rnd: *K1, ssk, knit to 3 sts before
marker, k2tog, k1, sm; repeat from * once more—
4 sts decreased.
Repeat Decrease Rnd every other rnd 5 times—
20 sts remain. Place 10 sts onto each of 2 needles. Using Kitchener st (see *Special Techniques*,
page 154), graft Top.

TOP-DOWN INCREASED

Increases worked at 2 points
Left/right interchangeable
Using Judy's Magic CO (see *Special Techniques*,
page 154), CO 20 sts. Join for working in the
rnd; pm for beginning of rnd.

Next Rnd: [K10, pm] twice.
Increase Rnd: *K1-f/b, knit to 1 st before marker,
k1-f/b; repeat from * once—4 sts increased.
Repeat Increase Rnd every other rnd 5
times—44 sts.

Complete Mitten as desired.

Decreases worked at 6 points
Left/right interchangeable
Work Lower Hand as desired, ending with 48 sts.

Note: *Beginning of rnd shifts by 1 st on Rnds 2 and 4.*

Rnd 1: *K5, s2kp2; repeat from * to end—36 sts remain.

Rnd 2: Remove marker, k1, pm for new beginning of rnd, knit to end.

Rnd 3: *K3, s2kp2; repeat from * to end—24 sts remain.

Rnd 4: Remove marker, k1, pm for new beginning of rnd, knit to end.

Rnd 5: *K1, s2kp2; repeat from * to end—12 sts remain.

Rnd 6: Knit.

Rnd 7: *K2tog; repeat from * to end—6 sts remain.

Break yarn, leaving a long tail. Thread tail through remaining sts, pull tight, and fasten off to WS.

PART 3

TECHNIQUES

The hallmark of all beautiful knitting is in the precise execution of its techniques. From the simplest decrease to exotic stitch patterning, all techniques require us to practice our understanding and implementation. You need to know both what to do and why. Fortunately for us, this part is fun! Whenever you are unsure of a technique, look for help from your knitting friends, in classes, and online, and practice, practice, practice.

Online technique videos can be really helpful when you need to see the actual motion of the yarn, needles, and hands. Just make sure you watch demonstrations from trusted sources, like well-known knitting teachers. I also recommend watching as many different versions of the same technique as you can find: There are often many ways to perform the same maneuver, and some will feel more natural to you than others. Constantly seeking to improve your understanding and performance of technique will make you a better knitter in everything you make.

Measuring

The warmest mittens are neither too snug (which could impede circulation) nor too loose (it takes time to warm up the extra space inside). Before you begin any mitten project, take the time to measure the hands you intend to cover. If your mittens are going to be a surprise for the recipient, try to sneak the measurements of a mitten that fits her or him. You can also consult the sizing table opposite to get a general idea. Precise measurements, along with accurate gauge swatch readings, will allow you to knit your mittens to exactly the size you need.

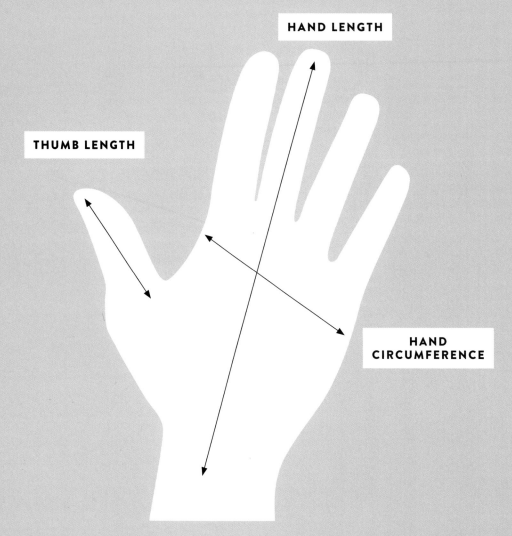

HAND LENGTH

THUMB LENGTH

HAND CIRCUMFERENCE

Hand Circumference: To determine the size you'll knit, hand circumference is the first thing you need to know. With the hand flat on a hard surface, place a flexible tape measure around the widest part of the hand (usually around the knuckles at the base of the fingers) and overlap the end without pulling too tight. Round this number to the nearest ½ inch (12 mm).

Hand Length: Place a tape measure or ruler with its end ("zero") perpendicular to the edge of a table. Use a piece of tape to hold it in place if needed. Now, rest the wearer's wrist right where the wrist bends on the edge of the table, on top of the ruler. Keeping the wrist in place on the edge, lay the hand down flat until the longest finger (usually the middle) rests flat on the ruler. Place another ruler, index card, or other straight object against the end of the longest finger and read where it lands on the ruler. Round this number to the nearest ½ inch (12 mm). This is the hand length.

Thumb Length: With the hand flat on a table, place the end of a ruler in the crook of the wearer's thumb. With the ruler's edge resting on the table and touching the length of the thumb, read the measurement closest to the tip of the thumb. Round this number to the nearest ¼ inch (6 mm).

STANDARD SIZE CHART

Once you have your measurements, use the chart below to determine the size you need.

	Baby 0–6 months	Child's X-Small 6 months–2 years	Child's Small 2–4 years	Child's Medium 4–6 years	Child's Large 6–8 years	Child's X-Large/ Woman's Small	Woman's Medium	Woman's Large/ Man's Small	Woman's X-Large/ Man's Medium	Man's Large
Hand Circumference	4" (10 cm)	5" (12.5 cm)	5½" (14 cm)	6" (15 cm)	6½" (16.5 cm)	7" (18 cm)	7½" (19 cm)	8" (20.5 cm)	8½" (21.5 cm)	9" (23 cm)
Hand Length	4" (10 cm)	4" (10 cm)	4½" (11.5 cm)	4¾" (12 cm)	5¼" (13.5 cm)	6" (15 cm)	6½" (16.5 cm)	7¼" (18.5 cm)	7¾" (19.5 cm)	8½" (21.5 cm)

Wearing Ease

Knitted fabric is a natural choice for mittens, because its ability to stretch perfectly accommodates the movements of hands. The snugness or looseness of the mitten fabric against the hand is described as "wearing ease."

Ease is expressed as positive, zero, or negative. Positive ease indicates knitting that is larger than the hand measurement. Zero ease describes knitting that is the same measurement as the hand. Negative ease defines knitting that is smaller than the hand, relying on stretch to fit. Most mittens are worked with zero ease; the knitting and the measurement are about the same, for a finished fit that is neither loose nor snug. Positive or negative ease is usually needed for knitted fabric with less or more stretch.

The amount of wearing ease you incorporate into your mitten is usually dictated by its style and the preference of the wearer. Typically, mittens intended to fit more loosely, such as thrummed or fulled styles, require positive ease. The Thrumpelstiltskin mittens on page 122 need extra wearing ease because the fluffy thrums inside take up space between the mitten and the hand. The Winter Garden mittens on page 134 and opposite require positive ease because fulling them reduces their ability to stretch.

Negative ease is needed for styles whose fit relies on the way they stretch around the hand. Fingerless designs such as Sporty Stripes (see page 110) or long designs such as Opera (see page 138 and opposite) require a closer fit to stay in place.

Whether positive or negative, the ease adjustment for handwear is usually slight. Adding or subtracting 5–10% should be plenty, and you can easily see what degree you prefer by fastening your gauge swatch around your hand with a safety pin if it's large enough. Once you determine the amount of ease needed, be sure to make note of it in your Mitten Design Worksheet (see page 19). Then, you can easily make adjustments to your stitch counts to accommodate it.

Gauge & Swatches

No knitting book is complete without the topic of gauge. Gauge refers to the number of stitches and rows in each square inch of knitted fabric. For a particular yarn, the more stitches you have per inch, the denser your fabric will be. Fewer stitches per inch will yield a more relaxed fabric. As the designer of your own mittens, you will be the final authority on what your ideal gauge is.

To determine this, swatching is required. Find a cozy spot to curl up and knit in, then do a little practice to make friends with your yarn. Try a number of different needles and knitting styles with the same yarn to see how you can alter the finished fabric. I recommend that you bind off each knitted swatch separately, rather than making one long one. This is because you will be working with small pieces of knitting, and getting an accurate measurement/stitch count can be harder when different gauges are adjacent in the same piece. To remember which swatch is which after washing and blocking, tie knots in the cast-on tail of each swatch corresponding to the needle size used, or make the same number of yarnovers, with corresponding decreases in the first few rows. If you make yarnovers, remember not to take your measurements in that area of the swatch, since the gauge will be affected.

For projects as small as mittens, a flat swatch is usually accurate enough. However, some techniques, such as entrelac or stranded colorwork, are more accurately swatched by knitting in the round. When in doubt, make your swatch by knitting a 6" (15 cm) circumference tube using the same needle configuration you'll choose for your mitten. You can even cut it open, so that it lays flat for measuring.

Multiple gauge swatches are useful for more than just measuring; you can also use them to learn how your yarn likes to be treated. When working with a new yarn, I like to make at least three separate swatches. I wash and block the first one according to the manufacturer's instructions. The second I treat as gently as possible; maybe only a light steam or spritz of water to find out if careful treatment makes the yarn more beautiful. The third swatch takes a beating: I've been known to machine-wash, hot-iron, or even sandpaper these in order to find out just how tough my yarn is. In the context of mittens, this can be really important—they are subject to greater abrasion than other knitted items. Don't fall in love with a yarn that can't take a little abuse in the finished mitten. The exception to this rule would be thumbless baby mitts—with those you can go crazy with the silk and cashmere, because they won't be treated the same way as kid or adult styles when worn.

When deciding on your gauge, remember that for mittens, a firmer gauge is almost always better than a more relaxed one. Take the manufacturer's recommendation into account, but remember that mittens need built-in resistance to pilling, excess stretching, and abrasion. These are all more easily avoided with a firmer fabric. Of course, you don't want your mittens to be too stiff and inelastic, so don't overcompensate. Let your swatches and your experience be your guide.

As illustrated by the Steampunkery Mitts below and on page 148, the same yarn worked at different gauges yields very different fabric types. Once you find the knitted fabric you like best for your mittens, measure it carefully. On a flat surface, use your ruler to count the number of stitches and rows in four inches (10 cm) of knitting, then divide by four. This is your final gauge in stitches per inch (2.5 cm). Plug the numbers into your Mitten Design Worksheet (see page 19) to proceed with your personal pattern.

Choosing Yarns

Consider the construction of your yarn to get the right result in your finished product. When making yarn selections and substitutions, here are a few things to keep in mind.

WEIGHT

The first characteristic to compare between the specified yarn and your substitution is its weight. Selecting a heavier or lighter yarn will result in a larger or smaller finished item, which can work to your advantage if you need to alter the size of a mitten without changing its actual stitch count. Swatch carefully to determine how much larger or smaller your knitting gets when you work with thicker or finer yarns and different needle sizes.

FIBER

The next thing to think about is the fiber your yarn is made of. Generally, fiber can be divided into three categories: natural, manmade, and blends.

Natural fibers come from either the trimmed coats of animals or from plants. Wool, cashmere, silk, and alpaca are all examples of natural fibers derived from animals. Cotton, linen, and hemp all originate from plants. Manmade fibers are derived from chemical mixtures made in textile factories. Examples of manmade fibers are acrylic, polyester, and nylon. Blends are combinations of different fibers in varying amounts,

which aim to provide the best traits of each. Blended fibers can be made from any combination of natural and manmade fibers.

Besides the way each yarn feels, an important consideration in choosing the fiber for your mittens will be how you intend to care for them. Some fibers, like cotton and superwash wool, are machine wash- and dryable, while others aren't. Some are delicate and require special care, like silk and cashmere, while others are durable and hardwearing, such as pure wool and synthetic blends. Think about how your mittens will be cared for (and by whom) as you consider the choices.

PLY AND TWIST

Another component of the yarn you choose is its construction. Yarn construction is defined by its ply and twist. The number of plies and the amount of twist will affect the way your knitted stitches look.

Fibers are held together in strands by twist. The tightness or looseness of the twist in each strand can influence its strength as well as the way the finished yarn looks and behaves. The individual strands of fiber in a yarn are known as "plies." Yarns that have

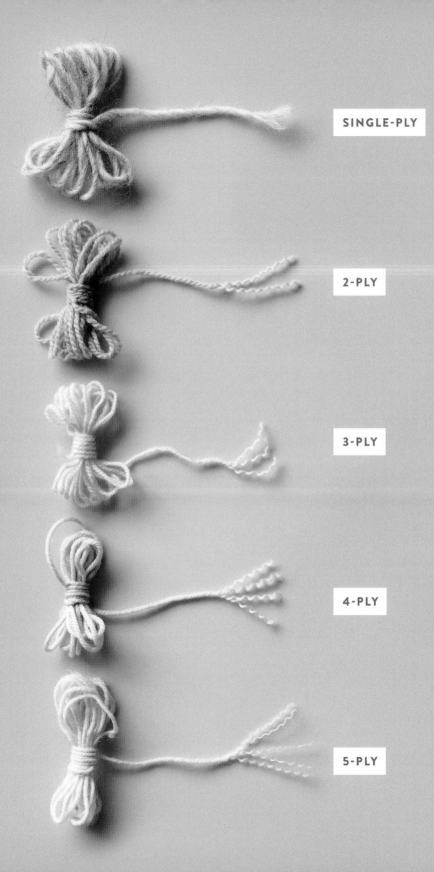

SINGLE-PLY

2-PLY

3-PLY

4-PLY

5-PLY

only one ply are known as "single-ply." Yarns with more than one ply are named after the number of plies they contain, such as "2-ply," "3-ply," and so on. Not all yarns specify the number of plies they have, but you can easily tell for yourself by separating the strands at the cut end of the yarn.

Note: *Older pattern and yarn sources, and some from the UK, refer to yarn weights by "ply." These references may not actually reflect the number of plies in the yarn. The only way to know for sure is to separate and count the number of plies in the physical yarn strand.*

Traditionally, ethnic and geographic mitten styles rely heavily on their indigenous yarns to achieve their finished look. Fair Isle styles use heathery 2-ply Shetland yarns. Scandinavian mittens look most traditional with high-twist, rounded 3-ply yarns. Ornate cables look best in heavy worsted- or Aran-weight yarn, which can have 3 to 5 plies. Consult the Patterns section beginning on page 66 to see examples of these traditional styles and the yarns used. Of course, it's not always necessary or practical to use traditional yarns for mittens, but it's good to know the reasons why these specific yarns were chosen in order to determine a good substitute.

COLOR

Of course, the colors you select will have an instant impact on your finished design. You can certainly pick the colors first and let that dictate your other yarn decisions. Just consider how the different colors will get along together in the finished mitten. Usually, yarns of similar weight, fiber content, and construction work together most effectively regardless of the colors you choose. If you're not sure how different colors from different manufacturers will behave together, swatch to find out. Often, yarns that look the same singly just don't work together cohesively. The best way to know for sure is to test them together in swatches.

One last thing to check for when choosing colors is dye transfer. When combining contrasting yarn colors, such as in stranded colorwork, always wash your test swatches to make sure one yarn won't bleed into the other.

Mitten Architecture

The components you combine to create your mittens and the method of their construction will determine their architecture. Different shaping techniques have evolved from knitting traditions around the world, knitters' experience with how to best cover different hands with different yarns, and the continuing evolution of our ideas about knitting. The menu of architectural choices presented here is based on my experience of mitten knitting and that of the many students I've met and worked with in my travels. Combined with your own body of knowledge and preferences, you've got a treasure trove of ideas and inspiration to work from.

DIRECTION OF KNITTING

Many mitten components lend themselves easily to being worked from any direction, while some are best worked one way only. The components you choose will help you decide how you'd like to construct your design. Other things to consider as you plan your knitting direction are the cast-on and bind-off you prefer, the stitch or color patterns you'll be working, and any finishing techniques you prefer or would like to try.

Before you start knitting, take some time to think about which type of construction is most suitable for the look you are trying to attain. Sometimes a better result can be achieved by changing the direction of your work. As in most knitting, the end result you desire will help you to determine the best way to get there. Here are some common ways to construct mittens:

FLAT
(Top-down, Bottom-up, Side-to-side)

Flat-knit mittens are worked in rows on only two needles, then sewn closed. Most commonly they are worked from the cuff to the top, but you could work in the reverse direction. If, for example, your chosen cuff edge treatment only works as a bind-off, working from the top down would be a good solution. Some of the oldest two-needle mittens are worked from side to side, typically in garter stitch. Examples of flat-knit construction can be found on pages 80 and 118. If you like the look of a flat-knit style but don't want the bulk (or work) of a sewn seam, consider working it circularly.

CIRCULAR
(Top-down, Bottom-up)

Circular mittens are seamless, and they are traditionally worked using double-pointed needles. Modern knitters also substitute two circular needles or Magic Loop needle configurations, depending on personal preference.

Note: *When deciding on your preference for needle configuration, remember that your gauge may differ from one setup to another. Practice and swatch before you commit to one and don't change from one to another mid-mitten or between mittens.*

Cast-on and bind-off techniques are often directional, meaning they work best from the bottom up or the top down. For example, if your favorite cast-on for 1x1 rib is worked from the bottom up and has no matching bind-off, you might decide to work your mitten from the wrist to the top. Conversely, if a decorative edge you love is only worked as a bind-off, you could choose to knit your mitten from the top to the wrist in order to incorporate it. Examples of top-down circular mittens are on pages 126 and 151, while those on pages 84 and 88 are worked from the bottom up.

TOP-DOWN VS. BOTTOM-UP

Stitch and color patterns can be fun to invert for different effects. Look at your favorite stitch dictionary upside down to see what I mean. If you elect to change a stitch or color pattern from top to bottom, look carefully at the charts as you work. Some chart symbols have to be changed from left to right when you flip them upside down in order to work properly. Practice by swatching them before you commit. Stranded colorwork patterns are also interesting when turned on their heads. Just make sure you look closely at how the actual stitches look upside down ("V" vs. "Λ"). You may find you have a preference or need to make small adjustments for the motifs to look their best. Again, when in doubt, swatch.

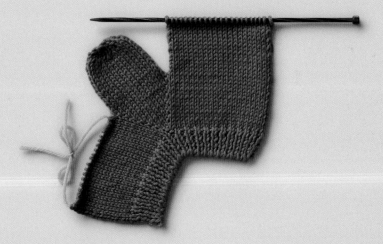

FLAT, BOTTOM-UP

FLAT, SIDE-TO-SIDE

The finishing required for mittens is usually minimal, which makes them an excellent canvas on which to try new techniques. For example, if you like the look of a toe-up sock cast-on, why not see how it looks on a mitten top? Just work your mitten from the top down to employ it. Top-down mittens also give you the advantage of trying on as you knit to find the perfect fit.

> **Note:** *Weaving in ends as you knit instead of leaving them for last is a fun and useful skill to learn. If working back and forth in rows makes doing this easier, knit your mittens flat, either from side to side, top to bottom, or bottom up.*

Changing the direction of your knitting can open whole new worlds of design ideas, so don't be afraid to experiment.

NEEDLE CONFIGURATION

Flat-knit mittens, regardless of the direction you work them, can be worked on straight needles. However, you can also work in rows using a circular needle, so don't reject flat-knit mittens just because you dislike using straight needles.

Circular-knit mittens are traditionally worked on double-pointed needles (dpns), in sets of either four (three needles in a triangle shape, using the fourth to move the stitches) or five (four needles in a square shape, using the fifth to move the stitches). If you are comfortable with this configuration, there's no reason to change. Just decide if your stitch count fits more logically into the four- or five-needle setup. Consider also the length and material of

your double-pointed needles. The needles you like best for sock yarn may not be your favorites for mittens, so don't hesitate to switch them out until you are comfortable. Double-pointed needles are also available in shorter lengths, specifically for mittens and gloves. You may find the shorter lengths more manageable, particularly when knitting fingers and thumbs.

Modern knitters have invented other needle configurations for creating small-circumference knitted tubes. If you don't like or don't have double-pointed needles, you can try working your mittens with two circulars, or using one long one for the Magic Loop technique. Some people find these configurations faster and more comfortable. Knitters switch from one needle to the next less often and more quickly with these setups. If you are experienced at knitting two socks at the same time on circular needles, definitely give two-at-a-time mittens a try. If knitting on double-pointed needles feels fiddly to you, or the ends poke your hands uncomfortably, audition other alternatives. Whatever your preferred needle configuration, make sure you have enough practice with it to accurately achieve the gauge you've decided on. And of course, if your gauge varies between one setup and another, make a note to use the same for both mittens.

Ultimately, the needles and configuration you prefer can usually be made to accommodate any knitting construction with a little creative thinking. Just keep experimenting until you're happy.

CIRCULAR, TOP-DOWN

CIRCULAR, BOTTOM-UP

PART 4

PATTERNS

Here is a collection of ready-to-knit patterns to inspire you. Spanning a variety of styles, constructions, and sizes, I've included a little of everything for you. If you'd like to change and customize them, everything you need is contained in this book. From simple to ornate, hardworking to refined, you'll find examples here to tickle your fancy and warm your heart and hands.

Lines & Ladders

Aran cables hold a special place in our knitting hearts, and the back of a mitten is a fantastic place to showcase a particularly beautiful one. In this ornate cable, the long gauntlet ribs represent ladders going down to the sea, while the intersecting cables stand for a fisherman's lines. The double-looped fringe at the lower edge adds an unusual touch.

SIZE
Woman's Medium

FINISHED MEASUREMENTS
7½" (19 cm) hand circumference

9½" (24 cm) long, including cuff, excluding fringe

YARN
Medium Weight

Sheepspot CVM Worsted [100% CVM wool; 280 yards (256 meters)/ 3½ ounces (100 grams)]: 1 skein Limestone

NEEDLES
One set double-pointed needles, or other needle(s) for working a small circumference in the round, size US 3 (3.25 mm)

Change needle size if necessary to obtain correct gauge.

NOTIONS
Stitch markers; cn; waste yarn; tapestry needle

GAUGE
24 sts and 38 rnds = 4" (10 cm) in St st

NOTES
These mittens are worked in the round from the bottom up. One size is given; the size may be adjusted by working at a firmer or looser gauge. See the worksheet on page 19 for instructions. You may work Cable Pattern from text or chart.

SPECIAL TECHNIQUES
See page 70

STITCH PATTERN
See page 73

COMPONENTS

LOOPED FRINGE CAST-ON, PAGE 27

WESTERN GUSSET THUMB, PAGE 43

SYMMETRICAL TOP, PAGE 48

LOOPED FRINGE CAST-ON

Wind yarn into a center-pull ball. Hold ends together and work with a doubled strand. Leaving a tail of approximately 3 yards (2.7 meters), make a slipknot and place it on the needle. Hold the yarn as for Long-Tail CO (see *Special Techniques*, page 154), making sure the yarn strands coming from the ball go over your index finger and the tail strands go over your thumb.

A. Pass the needle under the front strands of the loop formed by the thumb from left to right (just as for Long-Tail CO).

B. Pass the needle over all 4 strands of the index finger loop. The loop around your index finger will be the loop of fringe.

C. Leaving the loop around your index finger, pass all 4 strands through the thumb loop (the new st on the needle will have 4 strands), remove the loop from the thumb, and insert your thumb under the tail strands.

D. Use your thumb and forefinger to tighten the thumb loop around the new st; remove your index finger from the loop and insert it under the strands coming from the ball.

The tightness of the new st and the length of the loop can be adjusted by gently pulling on one strand or the other before making the next st. Repeat steps A–D for each CO st.

2/1 RC-P: 2 OVER 1 RIGHT CROSS, PURLED

Slip 1 st to cn, hold to back, k2, p1 from cn.

2/1 LC-P: 2 OVER 1 LEFT CROSS, PURLED

Slip 2 sts to cn, hold to front, p1, k2 from cn.

C4B: CABLE 4 BACK

Slip 2 sts to cn, hold to back, k2, k2 from cn.

C4F: CABLE 4 FRONT

Slip 2 sts to cn, hold to front, k2, k2 from cn.

LEFT MITTEN

EDGE

Using Looped Fringe CO, CO 52 sts.
Cut one of the strands coming from the ball, leaving a 6" (15 cm) tail. Trim CO tails to approximately 6" (15 cm).
Purl 1 row, working each 4-strand st as one st.
Join for working in the rnd, being careful not to twist sts; pm for beginning of rnd.

CUFF

Next Rnd: P2, [k2, p2] 8 times, [k4, p2] twice, k2, p2, k2.
Repeat last rnd 21 times.

SHAPE THUMB GUSSET

Increase Rnd 1: K24, pm for Thumb Gusset, M1R, k2, M1L, pm for Thumb Gusset, work Cable Pattern across 26 sts—54 sts.
Work 2 rnds even, working sts after second marker in Cable Pattern as established and remaining sts in St st.
Increase Rnd 2: Knit to marker, sm, M1R, knit to marker, M1L, sm, work to end—2 sts increased.
Repeat Increase Rnd 2 every third rnd 6 times—68 sts.
Work 2 rnds even.
Next Rnd: Knit to marker, remove marker, place 18 Thumb Gusset sts on waste yarn, CO 2 sts, sm, work to end—52 sts remain.

HAND

Work through Rnd 60 of Cable Pattern.

SHAPE MITTEN TOP

Decrease Rnd: K1, ssk, knit to 3 sts before marker, k2tog, k1, work to end, working decreases as indicated in chart—4 sts decreased.
Repeat Decrease Rnd every rnd 6 times—24 sts remain.
Using Kitchener st (see *Special Techniques*, page 154), graft Mitten Top.

THUMB

Transfer Thumb Gusset sts to needle(s); rejoin yarn.
Join for working in the rnd; pm for beginning of rnd.
Work in St st for approximately 1½" (4 cm).

SHAPE THUMB TOP

Set-Up Rnd: K9, pm, k9.
Decrease Rnd: *K1, ssk, knit to 3 sts before marker, k2tog, k1; repeat from * once—4 sts decreased.
Repeat Decrease Rnd every other rnd once—10 sts remain.
Using Kitchener st, graft Thumb Top.

RIGHT MITTEN

Work as for Left Mitten to end of cuff.

SHAPE THUMB GUSSET

Increase Rnd 1: Work Cable Pattern across 26 sts, pm for Thumb Gusset, M1R, k2, M1L, pm for Thumb Gusset, knit to end—54 sts.
Work 2 rnds even, working sts before first marker in Cable Pattern as established, and remaining sts in St st.
Increase Rnd 2: Work to marker, sm, M1R, knit to marker, M1L, sm, knit to end—2 sts increased.
Repeat Increase Rnd 2 every third rnd 6 times—68 sts.
Work 2 rnds even.
Next Rnd: Work to marker, remove marker, place 18 Thumb Gusset sts on waste yarn, sm, CO 2 sts, knit to end—52 sts remain.

HAND

Work through Rnd 60 of Cable Pattern.

SHAPE MITTEN TOP

Decrease Rnd: Work to marker, working decreases as indicated in chart, sm, k1, ssk, knit to last 3 sts, k2tog, k1—4 sts decreased.
Repeat Decrease Rnd every rnd 6 times—24 sts remain.
Using Kitchener st, graft Mitten Top.

THUMB

Complete as for Left Mitten.

FINISHING

Weave in ends, using tails to close gaps at base of Thumb. Block as desired.

CABLE PATTERN

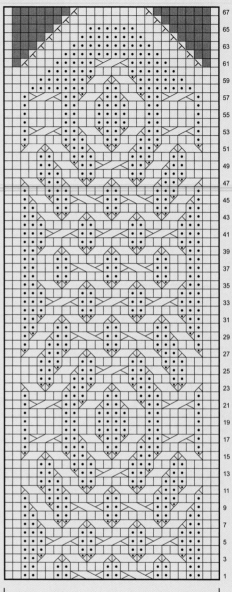

26-st panel; decreases to 12-st panel

	Knit		2/1 RC-p
	Purl		2/1 LC-p
	K2tog		C4B
	Ssk		C4F
	No st		

CABLE PATTERN (SEE CHART)

(panel of 26 sts; decreases to panel of 12 sts)

RND 1: [K2, p2] twice, [C4F, p2] twice, k2, p2, k2.

RND 2 AND ALL EVEN-NUMBERED RNDS THROUGH RND 56: Knit the knit sts and purl the purl sts as they face you.

RND 3: K2, p2, [2/1 LC-p, 2/1 RC-p] 3 times, p2, k2.

RND 5: K2, p3, [C4B, p2] 3 times, p1, k2.

RND 7: K2, p2, [2/1 RC-p, 2/1 LC-p] 3 times, p2, k2.

RND 9: K2, p1, 2/1 RC-p, p2, [C4F, p2] twice, 2/1 LC-p, p1, k2.

RND 11: K2, 2/1 RC-p, p2, [2/1 RC-p, 2/1 LC-p] twice, p2, 2/1 LC-p, k2.

RND 13: K4, p2, 2/1 RC-p, p2, C4B, p2, 2/1 LC-p, p2, k4.

RND 15: K2, 2/1 LC-p, 2/1 RC-p, p2, 2/1 RC-p, 2/1 LC-p, p2, 2/1 LC-p, 2/1 RC-p, k2.

RND 17: K2, p1, C4B, p2, 2/1 RC-p, p2, 2/1 LC-p, p2, C4B, p1, k2.

RND 19: K2, p1, k4, p2, k2, p4, k2, p2, k4, p1, k2.

RND 21: K2, p1, C4B, p2, 2/1 LC-p, p2, 2/1 RC-p, p2, C4B, p1, k2.

RND 23: K2, 2/1 RC-p, 2/1 LC-p, p2, 2/1 LC-p, 2/1 RC-p, p2, 2/1 RC-p, 2/1 LC-p, k2.

RND 25: K4, p2, 2/1 LC-p, p2, C4B, p2, 2/1 RC-p, p2, k4.

RND 27: K2, 2/1 LC-p, p2, [2/1 LC-p, 2/1 RC-p] twice, p2, 2/1 RC-p, k2.

RND 29: K2, p1, 2/1 LC-p, p2, [C4F, p2] twice, 2/1 RC-p, p1, k2.

RND 31: K2, p2, [2/1 LC-p, 2/1 RC-p] 3 times, p2, k2.

RND 33: K2, p3, [C4B, p2] 3 times, p1, k2.

RND 35: K2, p2, [2/1 RC-p, 2/1 LC-p] 3 times, p2, k2.

RND 37: [K2, p2] twice, [C4F, p2] twice, k2, p2, k2.

RND 39: K2, p2, [2/1 LC-p, 2/1 RC-p] 3 times, p2, k2.

RND 41: K2, p3, [C4B, p2] 3 times, p1, k2.

RND 43: K2, p2, [2/1 RC-p, 2/1 LC-p] 3 times, p2, k2.

RND 45: K2, p1, 2/1 RC-p, p2, [C4F, p2] twice, 2/1 LC-p, p1, k2.

RND 47: K2, 2/1 RC-p, p2, [2/1 RC-p, 2/1 LC-p] twice, p2, 2/1 LC-p, k2.

RND 49: K4, p2, 2/1 RC-p, p2, C4B, p2, 2/1 LC-p, p2, k4.

RND 51: K2, 2/1 LC-p, 2/1 RC-p, p2, 2/1 RC-p, 2/1 LC-p, p2, 2/1 LC-p, 2/1 RC-p, k2.

RND 53: K2, p1, C4B, p2, 2/1 RC-p, p2, 2/1 LC-p, p2, C4B, p1, k2.

RND 55: K2, p1, k4, p2, k2, p4, k2, p2, k4, p1, k2.

RND 57: K2, p1, C4B, p2, 2/1 LC-p, p2, 2/1 RC-p, p2, C4B, p1, k2.

RND 58: K3, p7, k2, p2, k2, p7, k3.

RND 59: K4, p6, 2/1 LC-p, 2/1 RC-p, p6, k4.

RND 60: K5, p6, k4, p6, k5.

RND 61: K1, ssk, k3, p5, C4B, p5, k3, k2tog, k1—24 sts remain.

RND 62: K1, ssk, k3, purl to last 6 sts, k3, k2tog, k1—2 sts decreased.

RNDS 63-65: Repeat Rnd 62 three times—16 sts remain.

RND 66: K1, ssk, knit to last 3 sts, k2tog, k1—2 sts decreased.

RND 67: Repeat Rnd 66—12 sts remain.

Littermates

Everybody knows that not all twins are identical. Like a fraternal twin, these mittens are the same, but different. A modern interpretation of Norwegian Selbuvotter, Littermates mittens feature knitted cord edges, snug ribbed cuffs, and pointed tops.

SIZE
Woman's Large/Man's Small

FINISHED MEASUREMENTS
8" (20.5 cm) hand circumference

9½" (24 cm) long, including knitted cord and cuff

YARN
Fine Weight

Brown Sheep Company Nature Spun Sport [100% wool; 184 yards (168 meters)/1¾ ounces (50 grams)]: 1 skein each #303 Sea Spray (**MC**), #103 Deep Sea (**CC1**), and #108 Cherry Delight (**CC2**)

NEEDLES
One set double-pointed needles, or other needle(s) for working a small circumference in the round, size US 3 (3.25 mm)

Change needle size if necessary to obtain correct gauge.

NOTIONS
Stitch markers; waste yarn; tapestry needle

GAUGE
30 sts and 32 rnds = 4" (10 cm) in stranded pattern

NOTES
These mittens are worked in the round from the bottom up. One size is given; the size may be adjusted by working at a firmer or looser gauge. See the worksheet on page 19 for instructions.

Where more than two colors appear in a given row (neck bows), work third color with MC, then work duplicate stitch with CC2 during finishing.

SPECIAL TECHNIQUE
See page 77

COMPONENTS

CORDED EDGE, PAGE 25

HORIZONTAL SLOT THUMB, PAGE 41

POINTED TOP, PAGE 45

LEFT MITTEN

KNITTED CORD

With CC2, CO 6 sts. K6; do not turn. *Slide sts to opposite end of needle, k6; repeat from * until cord measures 8" (20.5 cm).

Place sts on waste yarn.

With MC and beginning a few rows from CO, pick up and knit 60 sts along one column of Cord sts (there should be excess length at both ends of Cord).

Join for working in the rnd, being careful not to twist sts; pm for beginning of rnd.

CUFF AND HAND

Work Rnds 1–32 of Left Mitten chart.

Next Rnd (Rnd 33 of chart): Work in pattern to last 11 sts, k8 with waste yarn, transfer waste yarn sts to left needle, work in pattern to end.

Work to end of chart—4 sts remain.

MITTEN TOP

Break yarns, leaving a long tail of MC.

To close Mitten Top, remove needles from last 4 sts.

Use the tip of the tapestry needle or a crochet hook to pull left side st through right side st and thread MC tail through left side st.

Pull center back st through center front st and thread MC tail through center back st.

Fasten off to WS.

THUMB

Unpick waste yarn from Thumb and place sts onto needle(s)—16 sts.

Next Rnd: With CC2, *pick up and knit 1 st at corner, k8; repeat from * once—18 sts.

Join for working in the rnd; pm for beginning of rnd.

Work in St st until Thumb measures 2" (5 cm), or to ½" (12 mm) less than desired finished length.

SHAPE THUMB TOP

Set-Up Rnd: K6, k2tog, k1, pm, ssk, k7—16 sts remain.

Decrease Rnd: *Ssk, knit to 3 sts before marker, k2tog, k1; repeat from * once—4 sts decreased.

Repeat Decrease Rnd every rnd twice—4 sts remain.

Close Thumb Top as for Mitten Top.

RIGHT MITTEN

Work as for Left Mitten to end of Knitted Cord, reversing MC and CC colors.

CUFF AND HAND

Work Rnds 1–32 of Right Mitten chart.

Next Rnd (Rnd 33 of chart): Work 3 sts in pattern, k8 with waste yarn, transfer waste yarn sts to left needle, work in pattern to end. Work to end of chart—4 sts remain.

MITTEN TOP

Break yarns, leaving a long tail of CC1.

To close Mitten Top, remove needles from last 4 sts.

Use the tip of the tapestry needle to pull left side st through right side st and thread CC1 tail through left side st.

Pull center back st through center front st and thread CC1 tail through center back st.

Fasten off to WS.

THUMB

Complete as for Left Mitten.

FINISHING

Weave in ends, using tails to close gaps at base of Thumb.

KNITTED CORD

Unpick CO sts from Cord and place on needle.

Remove waste yarn from Cord end and unravel if necessary to fit Cuff, butting ends.

Using Kitchener st (see *Special Techniques*, page 154), graft Cord ends.

With CC2 and tapestry needle, work Duplicate st (see *Special Techniques*, page 154) where indicated on chart.

Block as desired.

SPECIAL TECHNIQUE

DUPLICATE STITCH

Thread a tapestry needle with chosen yarn, leaving a tail to be woven in later, *bring the needle from WS to RS of work at the base of the st to be covered, pass the needle under both loops (the base of the st above) above the st to be covered; insert the needle into same place where you started (base of st), and pull yarn through to WS of work. Be sure that the new st is the same tension as the rest of the piece. Repeat from * for additional sts.

A good way to visualize the path of the yarn for duplicate st is to work a swatch in St st using main color (MC) for three rows, work 1 row alternating MC and a contrasting color (CC), then work two additional rows using MC only.

LEFT MITTEN

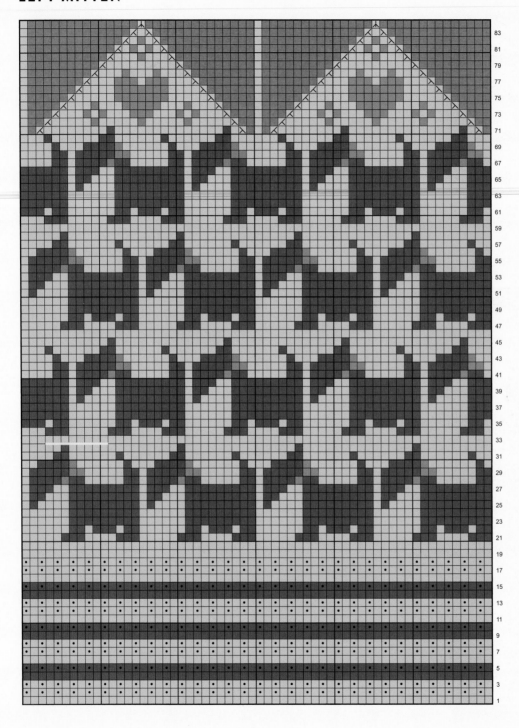

RIGHT MITTEN

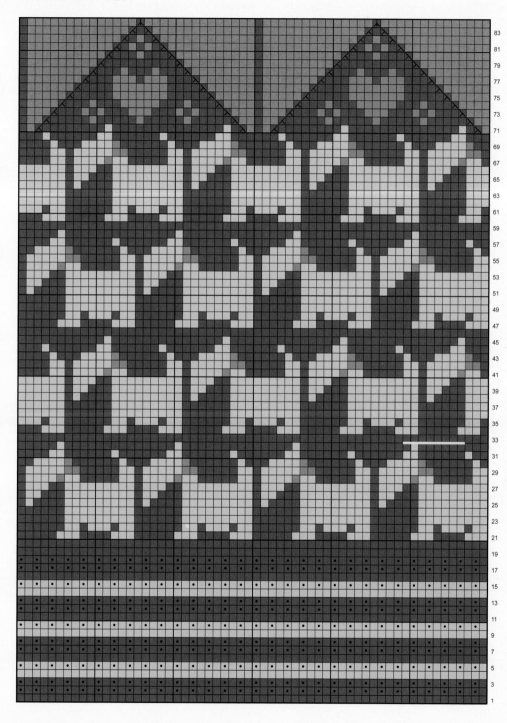

▢	MC
▨	CC1
▨	CC2
▨	No st
•	Purl
⟋	K2tog
⟍	Ssk
⋏	S2kp2
▬	thumb opening (waste yarn)

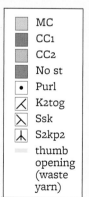

Blue Raspberries

This old-fashioned mitten style is delightful and quick to knit sideways. It's worked flat and seamed into shape at the end. The cuffs are snug, while the extra width of the hand is accommodated by simple short rows in the center of each. Garter stitch makes a cushiony and durable fabric, perfect for little ones. Bobbles worked at the side of the piece end up on the wearer's wrists, like a row of little berries.

SIZES
Child's X-Small (Small, Medium)

FINISHED MEASUREMENTS
5½ (5¾, 6¼)" [14 (14.5, 16) cm] hand circumference

6 (6¾, 7½)" [15 (17, 19) cm] long, including cuff

YARN
Medium Weight

Cascade Yarns Cascade 220 [100% Peruvian Highland wool; 220 yards (200 meters)/ 3½ ounces (100 grams)]: 1 skein #8908 Anis

NEEDLES
One set straight needles size US 6 (4 mm)

Change needle size if necessary to obtain correct gauge.

GAUGE
21 sts and 40 rows = 4" (10 cm) in Garter st

NOTES
Mittens are worked back and forth in rows from side to side in Garter stitch (knit every stitch, every row). The mitten begins at the outside of the hand, with increases and decreases to shape the tip and short rows to add fullness to the hand. Stitches are bound off for the side of the hand above the thumb, then stitches are cast on for the thumb. The thumb is shaped with short rows, then the thumb stitches are bound off and stitches for the side of the second half of the hand are cast on. The second half is shaped as for the first.

SPECIAL ABBREVIATION
MAKE BOBBLE (MB)
K1-f/b/f/b, [transfer 4 sts to left needle, k4] twice, pass second, third, and fourth sts over first.

SPECIAL TECHNIQUE
See page 83

COMPONENTS
(worked sideways)

BOBBLED EDGE, PAGE 27

WESTERN GUSSET THUMB, PAGE 43

SYMMETRICAL TOP, PAGE 48

MITTENS

FIRST HALF OF HAND

CO 28 (32, 36) sts.
Next Row (RS): Knit.
Next Row: MB, knit to end.
Increase Row: K1-f/b, knit to end—1 st increased.
Repeat Increase Row every RS row twice—31 (35, 39) sts.
Next Row (WS): MB, knit to end.
Repeat Increase Row—32 (36, 40) sts.
Knit 1 (1, 3) row(s).

Note: *Hand is shaped using Short Rows (see Special Technique, opposite page). It is not necessary to hide wraps when working Garter st.*

Short Row 1 (RS): K22 (24, 26), wrp-t.
Short Row 2 (WS): Knit to end.
Knit 2 (2, 1) row(s).

SIZE MEDIUM ONLY
Next Row (WS): MB, knit to end.

ALL SIZES
Repeat Short Rows 1 and 2.
Knit 1 (1, 4) row(s).

SIZES X-SMALL AND SMALL ONLY
Next Row (WS): MB, knit to end.

ALL SIZES
Knit 0 (2, 0) rows.
Decrease Row (RS): K2tog, knit to end—1 st decreased.
Repeat Decrease Row every RS row 2 (1, 0) time(s)—29 (34, 39) sts remain.
Next Row (WS): MB, knit to end.
Repeat Decrease Row every RS row 1 (2, 3) time(s)—28 (32, 36) sts remain.

SIZES X-SMALL AND SMALL ONLY
Next Row (WS): Knit to last 9 (11, -) sts, BO 9 (11, -) sts—19 (21, -) sts remain.

SIZE MEDIUM ONLY
Next Row (WS): MB, knit to last 13 sts, BO 13 sts—23 sts remain.

ALL SIZES
Break yarn.

THUMB

With RS facing, rejoin yarn and, using Cable CO (see *Special Techniques*, page 154), CO 6 (8, 10) sts onto left needle—25 (29, 33) sts.
Short Row 1 (RS): K8 (10, 12), wrp-t.
Short Row 2 and All WS Short Rows: Knit to end.
Short Row 3: K10 (12, 14), wrp-t.
Short Row 5: K12 (14, 16), wrp-t.
Short Row 7: K15 (17, 19), wrp-t.
Short Row 9: K12 (14, 16), wrp-t.
Short Row 11: K10 (12, 14), wrp-t.
Short Row 13: K8 (10, 12), wrp-t.
Short Row 14 (WS): Knit to end.
Next Row (RS): Knit.

SIZES X-SMALL AND MEDIUM ONLY
Next Row: Knit to last 6 (-, 10) sts, BO 6 (-, 10) sts—19 (-, 23) sts remain.

SIZE SMALL ONLY
Next Row: MB, knit to last 8 sts, BO 8 sts—21 sts remain.

ALL SIZES
Break yarn.

SECOND HALF OF HAND

With RS facing, rejoin yarn and, using Cable CO, CO 9 (11, 13) sts onto left needle—28 (32, 36) sts.

Next Row (RS): Knit.

SIZE X-SMALL ONLY

Next Row (WS): MB, knit to end.

SIZES SMALL AND MEDIUM ONLY

Next Row (WS): Knit to end.

ALL SIZES

Increase Row: K1-f/b, knit to end—1 st increased.

Repeat Increase Row every RS row 2 (1, 0) time(s)—31 (34, 37) sts.

Next Row (WS): MB, knit to end.

Repeat Increase Row every RS row 1 (2, 3) time(s)—32 (36, 40) sts.

SIZE MEDIUM ONLY

Next Row (WS): MB, knit to end.

ALL SIZES

Knit 1 (1, 2) rows(s).

Short Row 1 (RS): K22 (24, 26), wrp-t.

Short Row 2 (WS): Knit to end.

Knit 2 (1, 2) row(s).

SIZE SMALL ONLY

Next Row (WS): MB, knit to end.

ALL SIZES

Repeat Short Rows 1 and 2.

Knit 1 (4, 1) row(s).

SIZES X-SMALL AND MEDIUM ONLY

Next Row (WS): MB, knit to end.

ALL SIZES

Knit 0 (0, 2) rows.

Decrease Row (RS): K2tog, knit to end—1 st decreased.

Repeat Decrease Row every RS row 2 (0, 1) time(s)—29 (35, 38) sts remain.

Next Row (WS): MB, knit to end.

Repeat Decrease Row every RS row 1 (3, 2) time(s)—28 (32, 36) sts remain.

Knit 1 row.

BO all sts.

FINISHING

Fold mitten in half along center of Thumb with RS together. Sew seam from Cuff to Mitten Top. Sew seam along Thumb and Index Finger edges. Weave in ends. Block as desired.

SPECIAL TECHNIQUE

SHORT ROW SHAPING

Work the number of sts specified in the instructions, wrap and turn (wrp-t) as follows: To wrap a knit st, bring yarn to the front (purl position), slip the next st purlwise to the right-hand needle, bring yarn to the back of work, return the slipped st on the right-hand needle to the left-hand needle purlwise; turn, ready to work the next row, leaving the remaining sts unworked. To wrap a purl st, work as for wrapping a knit st, but bring yarn to the back (knit position) before slipping the st, and to the front after slipping the st.

Cactus Flower

Sometimes you just need a little pink! Pretty picots and palm gussets complement the perfect pink in this happy pair, just right for brightening the gray days of winter. You'll have enough yarn to make a third mitten, in case one gets lost.

SIZES
Child's X-Small (Small, Medium)

FINISHED MEASUREMENTS
5¼ (5½, 6)″ [13.5 (14, 15) cm] hand circumference

5¾ (6½, 7¼)″ [14.5 (16.5, 18.5) cm] long, including hem and cuff

YARN
Light Weight

Madelinetosh Tosh DK [100% merino wool; 225 yards (205 meters)/ 3½ ounces (100 grams)]: 1 skein Cactus Flower

NEEDLES
One set double-pointed needles, or other needle(s) for working a small circumference in the round, size US 6 (4 mm)

Change needle size if necessary to obtain correct gauge.

NOTIONS
Stitch markers; waste yarn; tapestry needle

GAUGE
23 sts and 32 rnds = 4″ (10 cm) in St st

NOTE
These mittens are worked in the round from the bottom up.

COMPONENTS

KNITTED PICOT HEM, PAGE 29

PALM GUSSET THUMB, PAGE 40

SYMMETRICAL TOP, PAGE 48

MITTENS

HEM

CO 30 (32, 34) sts. Join for working in the rnd, being careful not to twist sts; pm for beginning of rnd.

Knit 6 rnds.

Picot Rnd: *K2tog, yo; repeat from * to end.

Knit 5 rnds.

Fold Hem to WS along Picot Rnd.

Next Rnd: *Insert left needle into first CO st and k2tog (CO st and next st on needle); repeat from * for each CO st—30 (32, 34) sts remain.

CUFF

Purl 1 rnd.

Knit 1 rnd.

Purl 1 rnd.

Knit 2 rnds.

Next Rnd: *K2tog, yo; repeat from * to end.

Knit 2 rnds.

[Purl 1 rnd, knit 1 rnd] twice.

SHAPE PALM GUSSET

Next Rnd: K5, pm, k20 (22, 24), pm, k5.

Increase Rnd: Knit to marker, sm, M1L, knit to marker, M1R, sm, knit to end—2 Hand sts increased.

Repeat Increase Rnd every other rnd 4 times—40 (42, 44) sts.

Knit 1 rnd.

Next Rnd: Knit to second marker, remove marker, place next 10 Thumb sts on waste yarn, sm (this now marks beginning of rnd)—30 (32, 34) sts remain.

HAND

Work even in St st until piece measures approximately 2¾ (3½, 4)" [7 (9, 10) cm] from last purl rnd.

SHAPE MITTEN TOP

Next Rnd: K15 (16, 17), pm, knit to end.

Decrease Rnd: *K1, ssk, knit to 3 sts before marker, k2tog, k1; repeat from * once—4 sts decreased.

Repeat Decrease Rnd every other rnd 3 (3, 4) times—14 (16, 14) sts remain.

Using Kitchener st (see *Special Techniques*, page 154), graft Mitten Top.

THUMB

Transfer Thumb Gusset sts to needles; rejoin yarn. Join for working in the rnd; pm for beginning of rnd.

Work in St st for ½ (½, 1)" [1.3 (1.3, 2.5) cm].

SHAPE THUMB TOP

Next Rnd: [K2tog] 5 times—5 sts remain.

Break yarn, leaving a long tail. Thread tail through remaining sts, pull tight, and fasten off to WS.

FINISHING

Weave in ends, using tails to close gaps at base of Thumb. Block as desired.

Drop-Top

Like all the best convertibles, these are good for changing weather conditions. Sure, there are times when you need the top up, but isn't it nice to have options? Try them in dark tones or bright, candy colors like these. These are also a great place to showcase that special pair of buttons you've been saving.

SIZES

Child's X-Large/Woman's Small (Woman's Medium, Woman's Large/Man's Small)

FINISHED MEASUREMENTS

7 (7¾, 8¼)″ [18 (19.5, 21) cm] hand circumference

8¼ (8¾, 9¼)″ [21 (22, 23.5) cm] long, including cuff

YARN

Fine Weight

Brown Sheep Company Nature Spun Sport [100% wool; 184 yards (168 meters)/ 1¾ ounces (50 grams)]: 1 (1, 2) skein(s) #N87 Victorian Pink (**MC**); 1 skein #109 Spring Green (**CC1**); approximately 25 yards (23 meters) each #303 Sea Spray (**CC2**), #N54 Orange You Glad (**CC3**), and #N59 Butterfly Blue (**CC4**)

NEEDLES

One set double-pointed needles, or other needle(s) for working a small circumference in the round, size US 3 (3.25 mm)

Change needle size if necessary to obtain correct gauge.

NOTIONS

Stitch markers; waste yarn; tapestry needle; two 5/8″ (1.5 cm) buttons

GAUGE

26 sts and 36 rnds = 4″ (10 cm) in St st

NOTES

These mittens are worked in the round from the bottom up. The mitten top is picked up and knit from the back of the hand.

STITCH PATTERNS

1X1 RIB

(even number of sts; 1-rnd repeat)

ALL RNDS: *K1, p1; repeat from * to end.

TWISTED RIB

(even number of sts; 1-rnd repeat)

ALL RNDS: *K1-tbl, p1; repeat from * to end.

COMPONENTS

WESTERN GUSSET THUMB, PAGE 43

SPOKE TOP, PAGE 49

LEFT MITTEN

CUFF

Using CC2 and Tubular CO (see *Special Techniques*, page 155) or CO of your choice, CO 46 (50, 54) sts. Join for working in the rnd, being careful not to twist sts; pm for beginning of rnd. Work 1 rnd of 1x1 Rib.
Change to CC1.
Work in Twisted Rib until piece measures 2¼" (5.5 cm) from CO.

SHAPE THUMB GUSSET

Change to MC.
Next Rnd: K23 (25, 27), pm, M1, pm, knit to end—47 (51, 55) sts.
Knit 2 rnds.
Increase Rnd: Knit to marker, sm, M1R, knit to marker, M1L, sm, knit to end—2 sts increased.
Repeat Increase Rnd every third rnd 6 (6, 7) times—61 (65, 71) sts.
Knit 2 rnds.
Next Rnd: Work to first marker, remove marker, place 15 (15, 17) sts on waste yarn, remove marker, knit to end—46 (50, 54) sts remain.
Knit 8 rnds.

LITTLE FINGER

Next Rnd: K5 (5, 6) and leave MC attached for next Hand step, place 36 (40, 42) sts on waste yarn—10 (10, 12) sts for Little Finger.
Next Rnd: With CC4, k10 (10, 12), CO 2 sts over gap—12 (12, 14) sts.
Join for working in the rnd; pm for beginning of rnd.
Work in St st for ¾" (2 cm).
Work 2 rnds of 1x1 Rib.
Using Tubular BO (see Special Techniques, page 155), BO all sts.

HAND

Transfer 36 (40, 42) Hand sts to needle(s); rejoin MC.
Next Rnd: Knit to end, then pick up and knit 1 st in Little Finger CO st, pm for beginning of rnd, pick up and knit 1 st in Little Finger CO st—38 (42, 44) sts.
Join for working in the rnd.
Knit 3 rnds.
Break MC.

RING FINGER

Next Rnd: With CC1, k6 (6, 7), place 26 (30, 30) sts on waste yarn, CO 2 sts over gap, k6 (6, 7)—14 (14, 16) sts.
Join for working in the rnd; pm for beginning of rnd.
Work in St st for ¾" (2 cm).
Work 2 rnds of 1x1 Rib.
Using Tubular BO, BO all sts.

MIDDLE FINGER

Transfer 6 (7, 7) sts from beginning of rnd and 6 (7, 7) sts from end of rnd to needle(s)—12 (14, 14) sts; join CC3.
Next Rnd: K6 (7, 7), CO 2 sts over gap, k6 (7, 7), pick up and knit 2 sts in Ring Finger CO sts—16 (18, 18) sts.
Join for working in the rnd; pm for beginning of rnd.
Work in St st for ¾" (2 cm).
Work 2 rnds of 1x1 Rib.
Using Tubular BO, BO all sts.

INDEX FINGER

Transfer 14 (16, 16) Hand sts to needle(s); join CC2.
Next Rnd: K14 (16, 16), pick up and knit 2 sts in Middle Finger CO sts—16 (18, 18) sts.
Join for working in the rnd; pm for beginning of rnd.
Work in St st for ¾" (2 cm).
Work 2 rnds of 1x1 Rib.
Using Tubular BO, BO all sts.

THUMB

Transfer Thumb Gusset sts to needle(s); rejoin yarn.

With MC, pick up and knit 1 st at crook of Thumb—16 (16, 18) Thumb sts.

Join for working in the rnd; pm for beginning of rnd.

Work in St st for ½" (12 mm).

Work 2 rnds of 1x1 Rib.

Using Tubular BO, BO all sts.

MITTEN TOP

Using CC2 and Tubular CO or CO of your choice, CO 26 (28, 30) sts.

Work 1 row of 1x1 Rib.

Pick-Up Row: With MC and RS facing, working along row 4 rows below Little Finger, beginning at Index Finger end, pick up and knit 22 (24, 26) sts along back of Hand, then knit rib sts—48 (52, 56) sts.

Join for working in the rnd; pm for beginning of rnd.

Work in St st until Mitten Top measures 2 (2¼, 2½)" [5 (5.5, 6.5) cm] from Pick-Up Row.

SHAPE MITTEN TOP

Next Rnd: *K12 (13, 14), pm; repeat from * to end.

Decrease Rnd: *Knit to 3 sts before marker, s2kp2; repeat from * to end—8 sts decreased.

Next Rnd: *Knit to marker, remove marker, k1, pm; repeat from * to end.

Repeat last 2 rnds 4 (5, 5) times—8 (4, 8) sts remain.

Break yarn, leaving a long tail. Thread tail through remaining sts, pull tight to WS, but do not fasten off.

RIGHT MITTEN

Work as for Left Mitten to end of Thumb.

MITTEN TOP

Using CC2 and Tubular CO or CO of your choice, CO 26 (28, 30) sts.

Work 1 row of 1x1 Rib.

Pick-Up Row: With MC and RS facing, working along row 4 rows below Little Finger, beginning at Little Finger end, pick up and knit 22 (24, 26) sts along back of Hand, then knit rib sts—48 (52, 56) sts.

Join for working in the rnd; pm for beginning of rnd.

Work in St st until Mitten Top measures 2 (2¼, 2½)" [5 (5.5, 6.5) cm] from Pick-Up Row.

Complete as for Left Mitten.

FINISHING

BUTTON LOOP

Using tapestry needle and MC, bring yarn from WS to RS through Mitten Top, then take yarn to WS 1 st away from first st and draw it through until loop is long enough for button to fit through snugly.

Leaving a loop each time, bring yarn from WS to RS through first hole again, from RS to WS through second hole, then from WS to RS through first hole a third time, then pull until loops are the same length.

*Holding yarn to left of needle, insert needle under loops, then over yarn and pull snug, pushing each st tightly against previous st.

Repeat from * until you reach opposite edge.

Fasten off.

Weave in ends, using tails to close gaps at base of Thumb and Fingers. Block as desired.

Fold Mitten Top down (in open position) and sew button to cuff under button loop.

Guernsey

Look at all the texture you can create using only knit and purl stitches! The many plies and firm twist of traditional Guernsey yarn perfectly highlight this design from the British Isles. A Channel Island Cast-On and symmetrical top shaping frame the design, top and bottom.

SIZES
Woman's Medium (Woman's X-Large/Man's Medium, Man's Large)

FINISHED MEASUREMENTS
7¾ (8½, 9)″ [19.5 (21.5, 23) cm] hand circumference

8¾ (9, 9¼)″ [22 (23, 23.5) cm] long, including cuff

YARN
Fine Weight

Wendy Guernsey 5-Ply [100% wool; 245 yards (224 meters)/3½ ounces (100 grams)]: 1 ball #500 Aran

NEEDLES
One set double-pointed needles, or other needle(s) for working a small circumference in the round, size US 3 (3.25 mm)

Change needle size if necessary to obtain correct gauge.

NOTIONS
Stitch markers; waste yarn; tapestry needle

GAUGE
22 sts and 36 rnds = 4″ (10 cm) in St st

NOTES
These mittens are worked in the round from the bottom up. You may work Boxes Pattern and Diamonds Pattern from text or charts.

STITCH PATTERNS
See page 96

COMPONENTS

CHANNEL ISLAND CAST-ON, PAGE 28

WESTERN GUSSET THUMB, PAGE 43

SYMMETRICAL TOP, PAGE 48

LEFT MITTEN

Using Channel Island CO, CO 46 (50, 54) sts. Join for working in the rnd, being careful not to twist sts; pm for beginning of rnd.
Work 10 (14, 16) rnds of Seed st.
[Knit 1 rnd, purl 1 rnd] 3 times.
Knit 3 rnds.

SIZES WOMAN'S MEDIUM AND WOMAN'S X-LARGE/MAN'S MEDIUM ONLY

Increase Rnd: K0 (1, -), work Boxes Pattern for your size across 6 sts, work Diamond Pattern across 11 sts, work Boxes Pattern for your size across 6 sts, k0 (1, -), pm, knit to last 2 sts, pm, k1-f/b, k1—47 (51, -) sts.

SIZE MAN'S LARGE ONLY

Set-Up Rnd: Work Boxes Pattern for your size across 8 sts, work Rnd 19 of Diamond Pattern across 11 sts, work Boxes Pattern for your size across 8 sts, pm, knit to last 2 sts, pm, k2.
Work 1 rnd even, working sts before first marker in Boxes and Diamond Patterns as established, and remaining sts in St st.
Increase Rnd: Work to second marker, sm, k1-f/b, k1—55 sts.

ALL SIZES

Work 2 rnds even, working sts before first marker in Boxes and Diamond Patterns as established, and remaining sts in St st.
Increase Rnd: Work to second marker, sm, k1-f/b, knit to last 2 sts, k1-f/b, k1—2 sts increased.
Repeat Increase Rnd every third rnd 6 (6, 7) times—61 (65, 71) sts.
Work 2 rnds even as established.
Next Rnd: Work to second marker, remove marker, k1, place 15 (15, 17) Thumb Gusset sts on waste yarn, k1—46 (50, 54) sts remain.

Work 25 (23, 18) rnds even as established.

Decrease Rnd: *Ssk, work to 3 sts before marker, k2tog, k1; repeat from * once—4 sts decreased.
Repeat Decrease Rnd every other rnd 1 (2, 3) time(s)—38 sts remain.
Work 1 rnd even as established.
Discontinue Boxes Pattern; work these sts in St st.
Repeat Decrease Rnd on next rnd, then every other rnd once—30 sts remain.
Work 1 rnd even as established.
Discontinue Diamond Pattern; work these sts in St st.
Repeat Decrease Rnd on next rnd, then every other rnd once—22 sts remain.
Knit 1 rnd.
Using Kitchener st (see *Special Techniques*, page 154), graft Mitten Top.

Transfer Thumb Gusset sts to needles; rejoin yarn. Join for working in the rnd; pm for beginning of rnd.
Next Rnd: M1, knit to end—16 (16, 18) sts.
Work in St st until Thumb measures approximately 2 (2¼, 3)" [5 (5.5, 7.5) cm].

Next Rnd: K8 (8, 9), pm, knit to end.
Decrease Rnd: *K1, ssk, knit to 3 sts before marker, k2tog, k1; repeat from * once—4 sts decreased.
Repeat Decrease Rnd every other rnd once—8 (8, 10) sts remain.
Using Kitchener st, graft Thumb Top.

RIGHT MITTEN

Work as for Left Mitten to end of Cuff.

SHAPE THUMB GUSSET

SIZES WOMAN'S MEDIUM AND WOMAN'S X-LARGE/
MAN'S MEDIUM ONLY

Increase Rnd: K0 (1, -), work Boxes Pattern for
your size across 6 sts, work Diamond Pattern
across 11 sts, work Boxes Pattern for your size
across 6 sts, k0 (1, -), pm, k1-f/b, k1, pm, knit to
end—47 (51, -) sts.

SIZE MAN'S LARGE ONLY

Set-Up Rnd: Work Boxes Pattern for your size
across 8 sts, work Rnd 19 of Diamond Pattern
across 11 sts, work Boxes Pattern for your size
across 8 sts, pm, k2, pm, knit to end.
Work 1 rnd even, working sts before first marker
in Boxes and Diamond Patterns as established,
and remaining sts in St st.

Increase Rnd: Work to marker, sm, k1-f/b, k1, sm,
knit to end—55 sts.

ALL SIZES

Work 2 rnds even, working sts before first marker
in Boxes and Diamond Patterns as established,
and remaining sts in St st.

Increase Rnd: Work to marker, sm, k1-f/b, knit to
2 sts before marker, k1-f/b, k1, sm, knit to end—
2 sts increased.
Repeat Increase Rnd every third rnd 6 (6, 7)
times—61 (65, 71) sts.
Work 2 rnds even as established.

Next Rnd: Work to marker, sm, k1, place 15 (15,
17) Thumb Gusset sts on waste yarn, k1, remove
marker, knit to end—46 (50, 54) sts remain.

HAND AND THUMB

Complete as for Left Mitten.

FINISHING

Weave in ends, using tails to close gaps at base
of Thumb. Block as desired.

SEED STITCH
(even number of sts)

RND 1: *K1, p1; repeat from * to end.

RND 2: *P1, k1; repeat from * to end.

Repeat Rnds 1 and 2 for Seed Stitch.

BOXES PATTERN
(SIZES WOMAN'S MEDIUM AND WOMAN'S X-LARGE/MAN'S MEDIUM) (SEE CHART)

(panel of 6 sts; 4-rnd repeat)

RNDS 1 AND 2: P2, k2, p2.

RNDS 3 AND 4: K2, p2, k2.

Repeat Rnds 1–4 for Boxes Pattern (Sizes Woman's Medium and Woman's X-Large/Man's Medium).

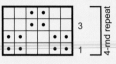

BOXES PATTERN
(SIZE MAN'S LARGE)(SEE CHART)

(panel of 8 sts; 4-rnd repeat)

RNDS 1 AND 2: [P2, k2] twice.

RNDS 3 AND 4: [K2, p2] twice.

Repeat Rnds 1–4 for Boxes Pattern (Size Man's Large).

DIAMOND PATTERN **(SEE CHART)**
(panel of 11 sts; 20-rnd repeat)

RNDS 1 AND 2: K5, p1, k5.

RNDS 3 AND 4: K4, p1, k1, p1, k4.

RNDS 5 AND 6: K3, [p1, k1] 3 times, k2.

RNDS 7 AND 8: K2, [p1, k1] 4 times, k1.

RNDS 9 AND 10: K1, [p1, k1] 5 times.

RNDS 11 AND 12: Repeat Rnds 7 and 8.

RNDS 13 AND 14: Repeat Rnds 5 and 6.

RNDS 15 AND 16: Repeat Rnds 3 and 4.

RNDS 17 AND 18: Repeat Rnds 1 and 2.

RNDS 19 AND 20: Knit.

Repeat Rnds 1–20 for Diamond Pattern.

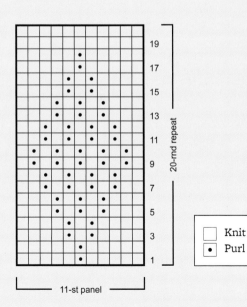

Leaves of Lace

These are mittens fit for a princess. A grown-up princess, that is. You could even add beads to the panels and cuffs. Why not? Lace is both magical and surprisingly warm to wear, but to make these extra cozy, you could knit a simple pair of cashmere liners to go with them—just the thing for Your Royal Highness.

SIZES
Child's Large (Child's X-Large/Woman's Small, Woman's Large)

FINISHED MEASUREMENTS
6½ (7¼, 8)" [16.5 (18.5, 20.5) cm] hand circumference
10 (10¼, 10½)" [25.5 (26, 26.5) cm] long, including cuff

YARN
Fine Weight

Abstract Fiber Chihuly DK/Sport [80% superwash targhee wool/20% silk; 740 yards (677 meters)/ 8 ounces (228 grams)]:
1 skein Big Girl Pink

NEEDLES
One set double-pointed needles, or other needle(s) for working a small circumference in the round, size US 4 (3.5 mm)
Change needle size if necessary to obtain correct gauge.

NOTIONS
Stitch markers; waste yarn

GAUGE
23 sts and 35 rnds = 4" (10 cm) in St st

NOTES
These mittens are worked in the round from the bottom up. You may work Cuff and Hand Patterns from text or charts.

STITCH PATTERNS
See page 101

COMPONENTS

WESTERN GUSSET THUMB, PAGE 43

GATHERED TOP, PAGE 48

LEFT MITTEN

CUFF

CO 84 sts. Join for working in the rnd, being careful not to twist sts; pm for beginning of rnd. Work Rnds 1 and 2 of Cuff Pattern 8 times.

Decrease Rnd: *K2tog; repeat from * to end—42 sts remain.

Work 8 rnds of 1x1 Rib.

Next Rnd: Knit, increasing 0 (4, 8) sts evenly to end—42 (46, 50) sts.

SHAPE THUMB GUSSET

Set-Up Rnd: K3 (4, 1), pm, work Hand Pattern for your size across 14 (14, 21) sts, pm, knit to last 2 sts, pm for Thumb Gusset, k2.

Work 1 rnd even, working sts between first and second markers in Hand Pattern as established, and remaining sts in St st.

Increase Rnd: Work to third marker, sm, yo, knit to end, yo, sm—2 sts increased.

Repeat Increase Rnd every third rnd 6 times—56 (60, 64) sts.

Work 2 rnds even as established.

Next Rnd: Work to third marker, remove marker, place 16 Thumb Gusset sts on waste yarn—39 (43, 47) sts remain. **Note:** *You will also have decreased 1 st in Hand Pattern on the previous rnd.*

HAND

Work 26 (26, 28) rnds even as established, ending with Rnd 10 (10, 2) of Hand Pattern—40 (44, 48) sts.

SIZE WOMAN'S LARGE

Next Rnd: Work to marker, sm, k2tog, yo, k1, k2tog, yo, k11, k2tog, yo, k1, k2tog, yo, sm, work to end.

ALL SIZES

Knit 0 (2, 1) rnd(s), removing all markers except beginning-of-rnd marker.

SHAPE MITTEN TOP

Decrease Rnd: *K2tog; repeat from * to end—20 (22, 24) sts remain.

Knit 1 rnd.

Repeat Decrease Rnd once—10 (11, 12) sts remain.

Knit 1 rnd.

Break yarn, leaving a long tail. Thread tail through remaining sts, pull tight, and fasten off to WS.

THUMB

Transfer Thumb Gusset sts to needles; rejoin yarn. Join for working in the rnd; pm for beginning of rnd.

Work even until Thumb measures approximately 1¼ (1½, 1¾)" [3 (4, 4.5) cm], or to ¼" (6 mm) less than desired Thumb length.

SHAPE THUMB TOP

Decrease Rnd: *K2tog; repeat from * to end—8 sts remain.

Knit 1 rnd.

Repeat Decrease Rnd once—4 sts remain.

Break yarn, leaving a long tail. Thread tail through remaining sts, pull tight, and fasten off to WS.

RIGHT MITTEN

Work as for Left Mitten to end of Cuff.

SHAPE THUMB GUSSET

Set-Up Rnd: K3 (4, 1), pm, work Hand Pattern for your size across 14 (14, 21) sts, pm, k3 (4, 2), pm for Thumb Gusset, k2, pm, knit to end.

Work 1 rnd even, working sts between first and second markers in Hand Pattern as established, and remaining sts in St st.

Increase Rnd: Work to third marker, sm, yo, knit to next marker, yo, sm, knit to end—2 Thumb Gusset sts increased.

Repeat Increase Rnd every third rnd 6 times— 56 (60, 64) sts.

Work 2 rnds even as established.

Next Rnd: Work to third marker, remove marker, place 16 Thumb Gusset sts on waste yarn, remove marker, knit to end—39 (43, 47) sts remain.

Note: *You will also have decreased 1 st in Hand Pattern on the previous rnd.*

HAND AND THUMB

Complete as for Left Mitten.

FINISHING

Weave in ends, using tails to close gaps at base of Thumb. Block as desired, pinning out points on Cuff.

1X1 RIB

(even number of sts; 1-rnd repeat)

ALL RNDS: *K1, p1; repeat from * to end.

CUFF PATTERN (SEE CHART)

(multiple of 14 sts; 2-rnd repeat)

RND 1: Knit.

RND 2: *K1, yo, k3, ssk, yo, sk2p, yo, k2tog, k3, yo; repeat from * to end.

Repeat Rnds 1 and 2 for Cuff Pattern.

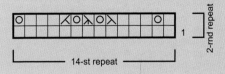

HAND PATTERN (SIZES CHILD'S LARGE AND CHILD'S X-LARGE/WOMAN'S SMALL) (SEE CHART)

(panel of 14 sts; 10-rnd repeat)

RND 1: Yo, k1, ssk, p1, k2tog, k1, yo, p1, ssk, p1, k2tog, yo, k1, yo.

RND 2 AND ALL EVEN-NUMBERED RNDS: Knit the knit sts and purl the purl sts as they face you; knit all yos.

RND 3: Yo, k1, ssk, p1, k2tog, k1, p1, sk2p, yo, k3, yo—13 sts remain.

RND 5: Yo, k1, yo, ssk, p1, [k2tog] twice, yo, k5, yo—14 sts.

RND 7: Yo, k3, yo, sk2p, p1, yo, k1, ssk, p1, k2tog, k1, yo.

RND 9: Yo, k5, yo, ssk, k1, k2tog, p1, k2tog, k1, yo.

RND 10: Repeat Rnd 2.

Repeat Rnds 1–10 for Hand Pattern (Sizes Child's Large and Child's X-Large/Woman's Small).

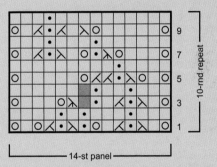

HAND PATTERN (SIZE WOMAN'S LARGE)
(SEE CHART)

(panel of 21 sts; 10-rnd repeat)

RND 1: K2tog, yo, k2, yo, k1, ssk, p1, k2tog, k1, yo, p1, ssk, p1, k2tog, [yo, k1] twice, k2tog, yo.

RND 2 AND ALL EVEN-NUMBERED RNDS: Knit the knit sts and purl the purl sts as they face you; knit all yos.

RND 3: K2tog, yo, k2, yo, k1, ssk, p1, k2tog, k1, p1, sk2p, yo, k3, yo, k1, k2tog, yo—20 sts remain.

RND 5: K2tog, yo, k2, yo, k1, yo, ssk, p1, [k2tog] twice, yo, k5, yo, k1, k2tog, yo—21 sts.

RND 7: K2tog, yo, k2, yo, k3, yo, sk2p, p1, yo, k1, ssk, p1, k2tog, k1, yo, k1, k2tog, yo.

RND 9: K2tog, yo, k2, yo, k5, yo, ssk, k1, k2tog, p1, k2tog, k1, yo, k1, k2tog, yo.

RND 10: Repeat Rnd 2.

Repeat Rnds 1–10 for Hand Pattern (Size Woman's Large/Man's Small).

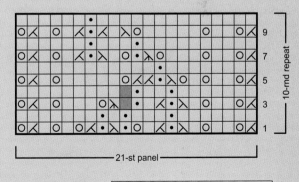

	Knit		K2tog
•	Purl		Ssk
	No st		Sk2p
O	Yo		

Little Birds

Many cultures celebrate the bluebird as a symbol of happiness. Here are some you can take along with you wherever you go. They're framed by Latvian Braids and accented by pretty palm thumbs and spiral tops. Little Birds will remind you in the gloomy days of winter that spring always comes, eventually.

SIZES

Woman's Medium (Woman's Large, Woman's X-Large)

FINISHED MEASUREMENTS

7¼ (8, 8¾)″ [18.5 (20.5, 22) cm] hand circumference

9 (9½, 9¾)″ [23 (24, 25) cm] long, including edge and cuff

YARN

Light Weight

Rauma Strikkegarn [100% wool; 115 yards (105 meters) / 1¾ ounces (50 grams)]: 1 (2, 2) skein(s) #101 Natural (**MC**); 1 skein #175 Bright Teal (**CC**)

NEEDLES

One set double-pointed needles, or other needle(s) for working a small circumference in the round, size US 3 (3.25 mm)

Change needle size if necessary to obtain correct gauge.

NOTIONS

Stitch markers; waste yarn

GAUGE

24 sts and 36 rnds = 4″ (10 cm) in St st

NOTE

These mittens are worked in the round from the bottom up.

STITCH PATTERN

LATVIAN BRAID

(even number of sts)

RND 1: *K1 with MC, k1 with CC; repeat from * to end.

RND 2: Move both strands to front of work. *P1 with MC, p1 with CC, bringing each strand up from **under** prior strand with every st; repeat from * to end (strands will twist around each other in this rnd, and untwist in the next one).

RND 3: *P1 with MC, p1 with CC, crossing each strand **over** prior strand with every st; repeat from * to end.

COMPONENTS

LATVIAN BRAID, PAGE 26

PALM GUSSET THUMB, PAGE 40

SPIRAL TOP, PAGE 46

MITTENS

EDGE

With MC, CO 44 (48, 52) sts. Join for working in the rnd, being careful not to twist sts; pm for beginning of rnd.
Work Rnds 1–3 of Latvian Braid.

CUFF

Work Rnds 1–6 of Lower Border chart.
Work Rnds 1–11 of Little Birds chart for your size.
Work Rnds 1–6 of Upper Border chart.
Work Rnds 1–3 of Latvian Braid.

SHAPE PALM GUSSET

Set-Up Rnd: K7 (7, 8), pm, knit to last 7 (7, 8) sts, pm, knit to end.
Increase Rnd: Knit to marker, sm, M1L, knit to marker, M1R, sm, knit to end—2 Hand sts increased.
Repeat Increase Rnd every other rnd 6 (6, 7) times—58 (62, 68) sts.
Knit 1 rnd.
Next Rnd: Knit to last marker, remove marker, place next 14 (14, 16) Thumb sts on waste yarn, sm (this now marks beginning of rnd)—44 (48, 52) sts remain.

HAND

Work even until piece measures approximately 7½ (8, 7¾)" [19 (20.5, 19.5) cm] from CO, or to 1½ (1½, 2)" [4 (4, 5) cm] less than desired Mitten length.

SHAPE MITTEN TOP

SIZES WOMAN'S MEDIUM AND WOMAN'S X-LARGE ONLY

Next Rnd: K6 (-, 9), k2tog, knit to last 9 (-, 12) sts, k2tog, knit to end—42 (-, 50) sts remain.

ALL SIZES

Set-Up Rnd: *K7 (8, 10), pm; repeat from * to end.
Decrease Rnd: *Knit to 2 sts before marker, k2tog; repeat from * to end—6 (6, 5) sts decreased.
Repeat Decrease Rnd every other rnd 5 (6, 8) times—6 (6, 5) sts remain.
Break yarn, leaving a long tail. Thread tail through remaining sts, pull tight, and fasten off to WS.

THUMB

Transfer Thumb sts to needles; rejoin MC.
Join for working in the rnd; pm for beginning of rnd.
Work even until Thumb measures approximately 1¾ (2, 2¼)" [4.5 (5, 5.5) cm].

SHAPE THUMB TOP

Next Rnd: *K2tog; repeat from * to end—7 (7, 8) sts remain.
Break yarn, leaving a long tail. Thread tail through remaining sts, pull tight, and fasten off to WS.

FINISHING

Weave in ends, using tails to close gaps at base of Thumb. Block as desired.

LITTLE BIRDS
(SIZE WOMAN'S MEDIUM)

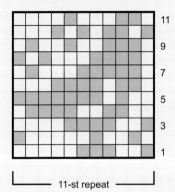

11
9
7
5
3
1

├─── 11-st repeat ───┤

LITTLE BIRDS
(SIZE WOMAN'S LARGE)

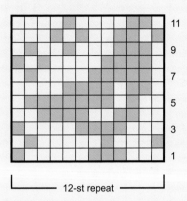

11
9
7
5
3
1

├─── 12-st repeat ───┤

LITTLE BIRDS
(SIZE WOMAN'S X-LARGE)

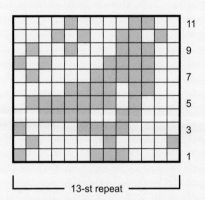

11
9
7
5
3
1

├─── 13-st repeat ───┤

LOWER BORDER

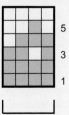

5
3
1

├─ 4-st repeat ─┤

UPPER BORDER

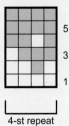

5
3
1

├─ 4-st repeat ─┤

| | MC |
| | CC |

Snow Day

Fair Isle knitting has such irresistible charm. Snowflakes in shades of blue and gray decorate these cuffs, reminding us of times when school got canceled and we played in the snow. Declare your own snow day, and give the drifts the attention they deserve.

SIZE
Woman's Large/
Man's Small

FINISHED MEASUREMENTS
8" (20.5 cm) hand circumference

10¼" (26 cm) long, including edge and cuff

YARN
Fine Weight

Harrisville Designs Shetland [100% Shetland wool; 217 yards (198 meters)/1¾ ounces (50 grams)]: 1 skein #49 Charcoal (**MC**); approximately 25 yards (23 meters) each #53 Silver Mist (**CC1**), #46 Oatmeal (**CC2**), #25 Aegean (**CC3**), #12 Seagreen (**CC4**), #10 Spruce (**CC5**), and #35 Chianti (**CC6**)

NEEDLES
One set double-pointed needles, or other needle(s) for working a small circumference in the round, size US 3 (3.25 mm)
Change needle size if necessary to obtain correct gauge.

NOTIONS
Stitch markers; waste yarn

GAUGE
27 sts and 40 rnds = 4" (10 cm) in St st

NOTES
These mittens are worked from the bottom up in the round. One size is given; the size may be adjusted by working at a firmer or looser gauge. See the worksheet on page 19 for instructions.

COMPONENTS

WESTERN
GUSSET
THUMB,
PAGE 43

SPIRAL
TOP,
PAGE 46

MITTENS

EDGE

Using MC and Tubular CO (see *Special Techniques*, page 155) or CO of your choice, CO 54 sts. Join for working in the rnd, being careful not to twist sts; pm for beginning of rnd.

Work Rnds 1–4 of Snow Day chart.

CUFF

Work Rnds 5–31 of chart.

SHAPE THUMB GUSSET

Change to MC.

Set-Up Rnd: K26, pm, k2, pm, knit to end.

Increase Rnd: Work to marker, sm, k1-f/b, knit to 1 st before marker, k1-f/b, sm, knit to end—2 sts increased.

Repeat Increase Rnd every other rnd 11 times—78 sts.

Knit 1 rnd.

Next Rnd: Knit to marker, remove marker, k1, place 24 Thumb Gusset sts on waste yarn, k1, remove marker, knit to end—54 sts remain.

HAND

Work even until piece measures approximately 9¼" (23.5 cm) from CO, or to 1" (2.5 cm) less than desired Mitten length.

SHAPE MITTEN TOP

Set-Up Rnd: *K9, pm; repeat from * to end.

Decrease Rnd: *Knit to 2 sts before marker, k2tog; repeat from * to end—6 sts decreased.

Repeat Decrease Rnd every other rnd 7 times—6 sts remain.

Break yarn, leaving a long tail. Thread tail through remaining sts, pull tight, and fasten off to WS.

THUMB

Transfer Thumb Gusset sts to needles; rejoin MC.

Next Rnd: M1, knit to end—25 sts.

Join for working in the rnd; pm for beginning of rnd.

Work even until Thumb measures approximately 1½" (4 cm), or to ½" (12 mm) less than desired Thumb length.

SHAPE THUMB TOP

Decrease Rnd: *K3, k2tog; repeat from * to end—20 sts remain.

Decrease Rnd: *K2, k2tog; repeat from * to end—15 sts remain.

Decrease Rnd: *K1, k2tog; repeat from * to end—10 sts remain.

Decrease Rnd: *K2tog; repeat from * to end—5 sts remain.

Break yarn, leaving a long tail. Thread tail through remaining sts, pull tight, and fasten off to WS.

FINISHING

Weave in ends, using tails to close gaps at base of Thumb. Block as desired.

SNOW DAY

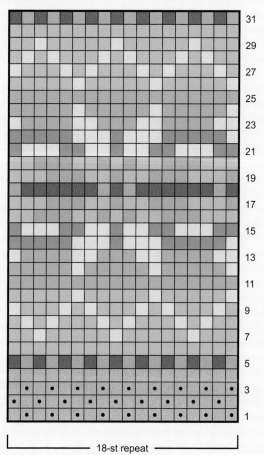

18-st repeat

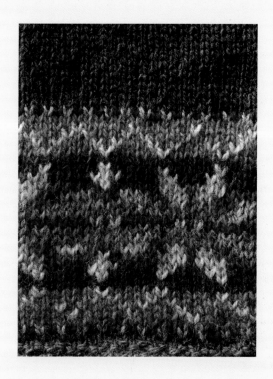

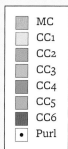
MC
CC1
CC2
CC3
CC4
CC5
CC6
• Purl

Sporty Stripes

Sporty Stripes mitts fit the shape of your hand by means of a clever trick: the palm stitches are worked in k2, p2 rib, continued up from the lower edge. You can actually make any mitten fit closer to the hand by employing this technique, but it's especially nice for fingerless styles that need to stay put.

SIZES
Woman's Medium (Woman's Large/Man's Small, Woman's X-Large/Man's Medium)

FINISHED MEASUREMENTS
7½ (8, 8¾)" [19 (20.5, 22) cm] hand circumference

6¼" (16 cm) long, including edge and cuff

YARN
Light Weight

Madelinetosh Tosh DK [100% merino wool; 225 yards (205 meters)/3½ ounces (100 grams)]: 1 skein each Aura (**MC**), Grasshopper (**CC1**), and Farmhouse White (**CC2**)

NEEDLES
One set double-pointed needles, or other needle(s) for working a small circumference in the round, size US 6 (4 mm)

Change needle size if necessary to obtain correct gauge.

NOTIONS
Stitch markers; waste yarn

GAUGE
22 sts and 32 rnds = 4" (10 cm) in St st

NOTES
These mitts are worked from the bottom up in the round.

STITCH PATTERN

2X2 RIB

(multiple of 4 sts; 1-rnd repeat)

ALL RNDS: *P2, k2; repeat from * to end.

STRIPE PATTERN
Working in st patterns as indicated, *work 5 rnds in MC, then 2 rnds in CC2; repeat from * for Stripe Pattern.

COMPONENTS

WESTERN GUSSET THUMB, PAGE 43

LEFT MITT

EDGE

With CC1, CO 48 (52, 56) sts. Join for working in the rnd, being careful not to twist sts; pm for beginning of rnd.

Work 4 rnds of 2x2 Rib.

CUFF

Change to Stripe Pattern.

Set-Up Rnd: K26 (28, 30) for back of hand, pm, knit to end for palm.

Working sts before marker in St st and sts after marker in Rib as established, work 13 rnds of Stripe Pattern, ending with 2 rnds of CC2.

Note: *When changing color for each stripe, knit all the stitches the first rnd, then work in St st and Rib as established to the next color change.*

SHAPE THUMB GUSSET

Set-Up Rnd: Continuing in Stripe Pattern, k2, pm, work as established to end.

Increase Rnd: M1R, knit to marker, M1L, sm, work as established to end—2 sts increased.

Repeat Increase Rnd every third rnd 6 times—62 (66, 70) sts.

Next Rnd: Place 16 Thumb Gusset sts on waste yarn, remove marker, CO 2 sts, work as established to end—48 (52, 56) sts remain.

HAND

Work 5 rnds even as established.

Change to CC1.

Knit 1 rnd.

Work 4 rnds of 2x2 Rib across all sts.

BO all sts in pattern.

THUMB

Transfer Thumb Gusset sts to needle(s); rejoin CC1.

Next Rnd: Pick up and knit 2 sts in crook of Thumb, knit to last st, ssk (last st of rnd and first picked-up st), pm for beginning of rnd—17 sts.

Next Rnd: K2tog, k1, p2, *k2, p2; repeat from * to end—16 sts remain.

Work 3 rnds of 2x2 Rib as established.

Loosely BO all sts in pattern.

RIGHT MITT

Work as for Left Mitt to end of Cuff.

SHAPE THUMB GUSSET

Set-Up Rnd: Continuing in Stripe Pattern, k24 (26, 28), pm, k2, sm, work as established to end.

Increase Rnd: Knit to marker, sm, M1R, knit to marker, M1L, sm, work as established to end—2 sts increased.

Repeat Increase Rnd every third rnd 6 times—62 (66, 70) sts.

Next Rnd: Knit to marker, remove marker, place 16 Thumb Gusset sts on waste yarn, CO 2 sts, sm, work as established to end—48 (52, 56) sts remain.

HAND AND THUMB

Complete as for Left Mitt.

FINISHING

Weave in ends, using tails to close gaps at base of Thumb. Block as desired.

Pearly Kings & Queens

Famous for their black suits elaborately decorated with pearl buttons, the Pearly Kings and Queens are England's original charitable organization. So intricate and complicated are their designs, Pearly clothes are often handed down from one generation to the next. These simple mitts are the perfect place to display your own pearl button collection. Worked flat with Seed stitch edges, the mitts feature gusset thumbs for a sleek and comfortable fit.

SIZES
Woman's Large/Man's Small (Woman's X-Large/Man's Medium, Man's Large)

FINISHED MEASUREMENTS
8½ (9, 9¾)" [21.5 (23, 25) cm] hand circumference

6¼ (6½, 7)" [16 (16.5, 18) cm] long, including cuff

YARN
Medium Weight

Plymouth Yarn Cashmere Passion [80% merino wool/20% cashmere; 164 yards (150 meters)/1¾ ounces (50 grams)]: 1 (1, 2) h(s) #0016 Purple

NEEDLES
One pair straight needles size US 8 (5 mm)

One set double-pointed needles, or other needle(s) for working a small circumference in the round, size US 8 (5 mm)

One pair straight needles size US 7 (4.5 mm)

One set double-pointed needles, or other needle(s) for working a small circumference in the round, size US 7 (4.5 mm)

Change needle size if necessary to obtain correct gauge.

NOTIONS
Stitch markers; waste yarn; removable markers; tapestry needle (optional; for Tubular BO); hand sewing needle and matching thread; fourteen ½"–⅝" (1.3–1.6 cm) mother-of-pearl buttons

GAUGE
22 sts and 30 rows = 4" (10 cm) in St st on larger needles

NOTE
These mitts are worked back and forth in rows from the bottom up.

STITCH PATTERN

SEED STITCH
(even number of sts; 1-row/rnd repeat)

ROW/RND 1: *K1, p1; repeat from * to end.

ROW/RND 2: Knit the purl sts and purl the knit sts as they face you.

Repeat Row/Rnd 2 for Seed st.

COMPONENTS

WESTERN GUSSET THUMB, PAGE 43

LEFT MITT

CUFF

Using smaller needles and Tubular CO (see *Special Techniques*, page 155) or CO of your choice, CO 42 (46, 50) sts.

Work 6 rows of Seed st.

Change to larger needles.

Work in St st until piece measures 2¼ (2½, 2¾)" [5.5 (6.5, 7) cm] from CO, ending with a RS row.

SHAPE THUMB GUSSET

Set-Up Row (WS): P13 (14, 15), pm, p1, pm, purl to end.

Increase Row (RS): Knit to marker, sm, M1R, knit to marker, M1L, sm, knit to end—2 sts increased.

Repeat Increase Row every RS row twice—48 (52, 56) sts.

Repeat Increase Row every fourth row 3 (3, 4) times—54 (58, 64) sts.

Work 1 WS row.

Next Row (RS): Knit to marker, remove marker, place 13 (13, 15) Thumb Gusset sts on waste yarn, remove marker, M1, knit to end—42 (46, 50) sts remain.

HAND

Work in St st until piece measures 5¾ (6, 6½)" (14.5 [15, 16.5] cm) from CO, or ½" (12 mm) less than desired Mitt length, ending with a WS row.

Change to smaller needles.

Work 6 rows of Seed st.

BO using Tubular BO (see *Special Techniques*, page 155), or in pattern using your preferred BO.

THUMB

Transfer Thumb Gusset sts to larger needle(s); rejoin yarn.

Next Rnd: M1, knit to end—14 (14, 16) sts.

Join for working in the rnd; pm for beginning of rnd.

Work in St st until Thumb measures approximately ½" (12 mm), or ½" (12 mm) less than desired Thumb length.

Change to smaller needles.

Work 6 rnds of Seed st.

BO using Tubular BO, or in pattern using your preferred BO.

BUTTON BAND

With smaller needles and RS facing, pick up and knit 42 (44, 46) sts along right edge of Mitt.

Work 6 rows of Seed st.

BO using Tubular BO, or in pattern using your preferred BO.

BUTTONHOLE BAND

With smaller needles and RS facing, pick up and knit 42 (44, 46) sts along left edge of Mitt.

Work 3 rows of Seed st, ending with a WS row.

Place 7 markers evenly spaced for buttonholes.

Next Row (RS): *Work to 2 sts before marker, k2tog, yo; repeat from * to 2 sts before last marker, k2tog, yo, work to end.

Work 3 rows of Seed st.

BO using Tubular BO, or in pattern using your preferred BO.

RIGHT MITT

Work as for Left Mitt to end of Cuff.

SHAPE THUMB GUSSET

Set-Up Row (WS): P28 (31, 34), pm, p1, pm, purl to end.

Increase Row (RS): Knit to marker, sm, M1R, knit to marker, M1L, sm, knit to end—2 sts increased.
Repeat Increase Row every RS row twice—48 (52, 56) sts.
Repeat Increase Row every fourth row 3 (3, 4) times—54 (58, 64) sts.
Work 1 WS row.

Next Row (RS): Knit to marker, remove marker, place 13 (13, 15) Thumb Gusset sts on waste yarn, remove marker, M1, knit to end—42 (46, 50) sts remain.

HAND AND THUMB

Work as for Left Mitt to end of Thumb.

BUTTON BAND

With smaller needles and RS facing, pick up and knit 42 (44, 46) sts along left edge of Mitt.
Work 6 rows of Seed st.
BO using Tubular BO, or in pattern using your preferred BO.

BUTTONHOLE BAND

With smaller needles and RS facing, pick up and knit 42 (44, 46) sts along right edge of Mitt.
Work 3 rows of Seed st, ending with a WS row.
Place 7 markers evenly spaced for buttonholes.

Next Row (RS): *Work to 2 sts before marker, k2tog, yo; repeat from * to 2 sts before last marker, k2tog, yo, work to end.
Work 3 rows of Seed st.
BO using Tubular BO, or in pattern using your preferred BO.

FINISHING

Weave in ends, using tails to close gaps at base of Thumb. Block as desired. With sewing needle and thread, sew buttons to button bands opposite buttonholes.

Lemongrass

One easy way to knit mittens is to work them back and forth in rows, then sew a seam. This pair highlights a thick, cushiony yarn in a special color. One elegant cable and a spiral top make these equally appealing for men and women. The fact that they also knit up in a flash makes them perfect for gift giving, too.

SIZES
Woman's Large/Man's Small (Man's Large)

FINISHED MEASUREMENTS
8 (9)″ [20.5 (23) cm] hand circumference

8½ (9)″ [21.5 (23) cm] long, including cuff

YARN
Medium Weight

Brown Sheep Shepherd's Shades [100% wool; 131 yards (120 meters)/ 3½ ounces (100 grams)]: 1 (2) skein(s) #SS573 Wintergreen

NEEDLES
One pair straight needles size US 8 (5 mm)

Change needle size if necessary to obtain correct gauge.

NOTIONS
Stitch markers; cn; waste yarn

GAUGE
17 sts and 26 rows = 4″ (10 cm) in St st

NOTES
These mittens are worked from the bottom up, back and forth in rows. Two sizes are given for this yarn, but many sizes can be made by changing the yarn and gauge. See the worksheet on page 19 for instructions. You may work Left and Right Cable Patterns from text or charts.

ABBREVIATIONS

C6F: CABLE 6 FRONT

Slip 3 sts to cn, hold to front, k3, k3 from cn.

C6B: CABLE 6 BACK

Slip 3 sts to cn, hold to back, k3, k3 from cn.

STITCH PATTERNS

1X1 RIB

(even number of sts; 1-row repeat)

ALL ROWS: *K1, p1; repeat from * to end.

LEFT CABLE PATTERN

See page 120

RIGHT CABLE PATTERN

See page 121

COMPONENTS

WESTERN GUSSET THUMB, PAGE 43

SPIRAL TOP, PAGE 46

LEFT MITTEN

CUFF

Using Tubular CO (see *Special Techniques*, page 155) or CO of your choice, CO 40 (44) sts.
Work 2 rows of 1x1 Rib, ending with a WS row.
Set-Up Row (RS): K24 (27), pm, work Right Cable Pattern across 10 sts, pm, k6 (7).
Work as established until piece measures approximately 2¾ (3¼)" [7 (8.5) cm] from CO, ending with a RS row.

SHAPE THUMB GUSSET

Set-Up Row (WS): Work 20 (22) sts, pm for Thumb Gusset, p1, pm for Thumb Gusset, work to end.
Increase Row (RS): Work to Thumb Gusset marker, sm, M1R, knit to marker, M1L, sm, work as established to end—2 sts increased.
Repeat Increase Row every RS row 6 times—54 (58) sts.
Work 1 WS row even as established.
Next Row (RS): Work to Thumb Gusset marker, remove marker, place 15 Thumb Gusset sts on waste yarn, remove marker, CO 1 st, work as established to end—40 (44) sts remain.

HAND

Work even as established until piece measures approximately 7¾ (8¼)" [19.5 (21) cm] from CO, or to ¾" (2 cm) less than desired Mitten length, ending with a WS row.

SHAPE MITTEN TOP

Decrease Row (RS): *K2, k2tog (or p2tog if second st of decrease is a purl st); repeat from * to end—30 (33) sts remain.
Work 1 WS row.
Decrease Row: *K1, k2tog (or p2tog if second st of decrease is a purl st); repeat from * to end—20 (22) sts remain.
Work 1 WS row.
Decrease Row: *K2tog; repeat from * to end—10 (11) sts remain.
Break yarn, leaving a long tail. Thread tail through remaining sts, pull tight, and fasten off to WS.

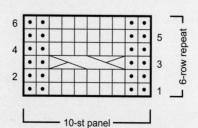

STITCH PATTERN

LEFT CABLE PATTERN (SEE CHART)
(panel of 10 sts; 6-row repeat)
ROWS 1 AND 5 (RS): P2, k6, p2.
ROWS 2 AND 4: K2, p6, k2.
ROW 3: P2, C6F, p2.
ROW 6: Repeat Row 2.
Repeat Rows 1–6 for Left Cable Pattern.

6-row repeat

10-st panel

Knit on RS, purl on WS.

• Purl on RS, knit on WS.

C6F

THUMB

Transfer Thumb Gusset sts to needle(s); rejoin yarn.

Next Row (RS): Pick up and knit 1 st in CO st, knit to end—16 sts.

Work in St st until Thumb measures approximately 1¼ (1½)" [3 (4) cm], or to ½" (12 mm) less than desired Thumb length, ending with a WS row.

SHAPE THUMB TOP

Decrease Row (RS): *K2, k2tog; repeat from * to end—12 sts remain.

Work 1 WS row.

Decrease Row: *K2tog; repeat from * to end—6 sts remain.

Break yarn, leaving a long tail. Thread tail through remaining sts and pull tight. Sew Thumb seam, then fasten off to WS.

RIGHT MITTEN

CUFF

Using Tubular CO (see *Special Techniques*, page 155) or CO of your choice, CO 40 (44) sts.

Work 2 rows of 1x1 Rib, ending with a WS row.

Set-Up Row (RS): K6 (7), pm, work Left Cable Pattern across 10 sts, pm, k24 (27).

Work as established until piece measures approximately 2¾ (3¼)" [7 (8.5) cm] from CO, ending with a RS row.

SHAPE THUMB GUSSET

Set-Up Row (WS): Work 19 (21) sts as established, pm for Thumb Gusset, p1, pm for Thumb Gusset, work to end.

Increase Row (RS): Work as established to Thumb Gusset marker, sm, M1R, knit to marker, M1L, sm, work to end—2 sts increased.

Repeat Increase Row every RS row 6 times—54 (58) sts.

Work 1 WS row even as established.

Next Row (RS): Work as established to Thumb Gusset marker, remove marker, place 15 Thumb Gusset sts on waste yarn, remove marker, CO 1 st, work to end—40 (44) sts remain.

HAND AND THUMB

Complete as for Left Mitten.

FINISHING

Sew Hand seam. Block as desired.

STITCH PATTERN

RIGHT CABLE PATTERN (SEE CHART)
(panel of 10 sts; 6-row repeat)

ROWS 1 AND 5 (RS): P2, k6, p2.

ROWS 2 AND 4: K2, p6, k2.

ROW 3: P2, C6B, p2.

ROW 6: Repeat Row 2.

Repeat Rows 1–6 for Right Cable Pattern.

6-row repeat

10-st panel

	Knit on RS, purl on WS.
•	Purl on RS, knit on WS.
⧄	C6B

Thrumpelstiltskin

Loved in Canada and throughout cold climates of the western hemisphere, thrummed mittens keep us warm with their unique fabric. Short lengths of unspun wool roving are incorporated into the knitting at regular intervals to create a lofty lining. These are the warmest of warm mittens, worked at a big gauge and filled with fluff! Who says you can't spin straw into gold?

SIZES

Woman's X-Large/Man's Medium (Man's Large, Man's X-Large)

FINISHED MEASUREMENTS

8½ (9½, 10½)" [21.5 (24, 26.5 cm] interior hand circumference

9 (9¾, 10½)" [23 (25, 26.5) cm] long, including hem

YARN

Medium Weight

Sheepspot CVM Worsted [100% CVM wool; 280 yards (256 meters)/3½ ounces (100 grams)]: 1 skein each Shale (**MC**) and Coralish (**CC**)

Sheepspot CVM Roving [100% CVM wool; 4 ounces (114 grams)]: 1 braid Invert

NEEDLES

One set double-pointed needles, or other needle(s) for working a small circumference in the round, size US 8 (5 mm)

Change needle size if necessary to obtain correct gauge.

NOTIONS

Stitch markers; waste yarn; tapestry needle

GAUGE

16 sts and 24 rnds = 4" (10 cm) in Thrummed St st with 2 strands of yarn held together

NOTES

These mittens are worked in the round from the bottom up. Work with two strands of yarn held together throughout.

To make thrums: Pull roving apart into 6" (15 cm) lengths. Strip each length into ¼" (6 mm) wide pieces. Fold each piece around three fingers, overlapping ends. Roll between hands to make thrum.

STITCH PATTERNS

See page 124

COMPONENTS

KNITTED PICOT HEM, PAGE 29

LATVIAN BRAID, PAGE 26

WESTERN GUSSET THUMB, PAGE 43

POINTED TOP, PAGE 45

LATVIAN BRAID

(even number of sts)

RND 1: *K1 with MC, k1 with CC; repeat from * to end.

RND 2: Move both strands to front of work. *P1 with MC, p1 with CC, bringing each strand up from **under** prior strand with every st; repeat from * to end (strands will twist around each other in this rnd, and untwist in the next one).

RND 3: *P1 with MC, p1 with CC, crossing each strand **over** prior strand with every st; repeat from * to end.

THRUM 1

Insert right needle into next st, wrap thrum around needle and pull through; strand MC over thrum. In next rnd, work thrum as a st, pulling ends snug on WS.

THRUMMED STOCKINETTE STITCH

(multiple of 4 sts; 8-rnd repeat)

RNDS 1–3: Knit.

RND 4: K1, *Thrum 1, k3; repeat from * to last 3 sts, Thrum 1, k2.

RNDS 5–7: Knit.

RND 8: *K3, Thrum 1; repeat from * to end.

Repeat Rnds 1–8 for Thrummed Stockinette Stitch.

MITTENS

HEM

With 2 strands of CC held together, CO 40 (44, 48) sts. Join for working in the rnd, being careful not to twist sts; pm for beginning of rnd.
Knit 6 rnds.
Picot Rnd: *P2tog, yo; repeat from * to end.
Knit 1 rnd.
Change to 2 strands of MC held together.
Knit 5 rnds.
Fold hem to WS along Picot Rnd.
Next Rnd: *Insert left needle into first CO st and k2tog (CO st and next st on needle); repeat from * for each CO st—40 (44, 48) sts remain.
Work Rnds 1–3 of Latvian Braid.

SHAPE THUMB GUSSET

Change to Thrummed St st.
Increase Rnd 1: Work 20 (22, 24) sts in pattern, pm, M1L, pm, continue in pattern to end—41 (45, 49) sts.
Work 1 rnd even.
Increase Rnd 2: Work to marker, sm, M1R, work to marker, M1L, sm, work to end—2 sts increased.
Repeat Increase Rnd 2 every other rnd 7 times, working new sts into Thrummed St st pattern—57 (61, 65) sts.
Work 1 rnd even.
Next Rnd: Work to marker, remove marker, place 17 Thumb Gusset sts on waste yarn, remove marker, work to end—40 (44, 48) sts remain.

HAND

Work even until piece measures 7¼ (8, 8½)" [18.5 (20.5, 21.5) cm] from Picot Rnd, or to 1¾ (1¾, 2)" [4.5 (4.5, 5) cm] less than desired Mitten length.

SHAPE MITTEN TOP

Set-Up Rnd: Work 20 (22, 24) sts, pm, work to end.
Decrease Rnd: *K1, ssk, work to 2 sts before marker, k2tog; repeat from * to end—4 sts decreased.
Repeat Decrease Rnd every rnd 8 (9, 10) times—4 sts remain.
Break yarn, leaving a long tail.
To close Mitten Top, remove needles from last 4 sts.
Use the tip of the tapestry needle or a crochet hook to pull left side st through right side st and thread tail through left side st.
Pull center back st through center front st and thread tail through center back st.
Fasten off to WS.

THUMB

Transfer Thumb Gusset sts to needles; rejoin 2 strands of MC held together.
Join for working in the rnd; pm for beginning of rnd.
Work in pattern until Thumb measures approximately 1½ (2, 2½)" [4 (5, 6.5) cm].

SHAPE THUMB TOP

Decrease Rnd: *K2tog, k1; repeat from * to last 2 sts, k2tog—11 sts remain.
Work 1 rnd even.
Decrease Rnd: *K2tog; repeat from * to last st, k1—6 sts remain.
Break yarn, leaving a long tail. Thread tail through remaining sts, pull tight, and fasten off to WS.

FINISHING

Weave in ends, using tails to close gaps at base of Thumb. Block as desired.

Topsy Turvy

Why knit your mittens from the top down? Because you can. Because toe-up cast-ons aren't just for socks, and they're fun. Because sometimes you want a mitten that fits with extreme precision. Because maybe the lower edge treatment you love works best as a bind-off. Because it's Tuesday and Mercury is in retrograde. You have your reasons.

SIZES
Woman's Medium
(Woman's X-Large/Man's
Medium, Man's Large)

**FINISHED
MEASUREMENTS**
7½ (8½, 9¼)"
[19 (21.5, 23.5) cm] hand
circumference

8¾ (9¼, 9½)"
[22 (23.5, 24) cm] long,
including cuff

YARN
Medium Weight

Jill Draper Makes Stuff
Windham [100% American-
grown merino wool;
220 yards (201 meters)/
4 ounces (113 grams)]:
1 skein Golden Delicious

NEEDLES
One set double-pointed
needles, or other needle(s)
for working a small
circumference in the
round, size US 6 (4 mm)
*Change needle size if
necessary to obtain correct
gauge.*

NOTIONS
Stitch markers; waste yarn

GAUGE
21 sts and 31 rnds = 4"
(10 cm) in St st

NOTES
*These mittens are worked
from the top down in the
round. You may work Left
and Right Cuff Patterns
from text or charts.*

ABBREVIATIONS

LC: LEFT CROSS
Insert needle from back
to front between first and
second sts on left-hand
needle and knit the second
st through the front loop.
Knit first st; slip both sts
from left-hand needle
together.

RC: RIGHT CROSS
Insert tip of right-hand
needle into front of second
st, bringing tip to front of
work between second and
first sts, knit st, knit first
st through front loop, slip
both sts from left-hand
needle together.

STITCH PATTERNS
See pages 128–129

COMPONENTS

WESTERN
GUSSET
THUMB,
PAGE 43

TOP-DOWN
INCREASED,
PAGE 48

LEFT MITTEN

MITTEN TOP

Using Judy's Magic CO (see *Special Techniques*, page 154), CO 24 sts.

Join for working in the rnd; pm for beginning of rnd.

Set-Up Rnd: K12, pm, k12.

Increase Rnd: *K1, M1R, knit to 1 st before marker, M1L, k1; repeat from * once—4 sts increased.

Repeat Increase Rnd every other rnd 3 (4, 5) times—40 (44, 48) sts.

HAND

Work even until piece measures approximately 4¼ (4¾, 5)" [11 (12, 12.5) cm] from CO, or to 4½" (11.5 cm) less than desired Mitten length (approximately the crook of your thumb). Place sts on waste yarn.

THUMB TOP

Using Judy's Magic CO, CO 8 sts.

Join for working in the rnd; pm for beginning of rnd.

Set-Up Rnd: K4, pm, k4.

Increase Rnd: *K1, M1R, knit to 1 st before marker, M1L, k1; repeat from * once—4 sts increased.

Repeat Increase Rnd every other rnd once—16 sts.

THUMB

Work even until piece measures approximately 2 (2¼, 2¾)" [5 (5.5, 7) cm] from CO.

Break yarn.

STITCH PATTERN

LEFT CUFF PATTERN (SEE CHART)
(multiple of 3 sts; 4-rnd repeat)

RND 1: *K2, p1; repeat from * to end.

RND 2: *LC, p1; repeat from * to end.

RNDS 3 AND 4: Repeat Rnd 1.

Repeat Rnds 1–4 for Left Cuff Pattern.

Knit
Purl
LC

JOIN HAND AND THUMB

Transfer Hand sts to needle(s); rejoin yarn.

Joining Rnd: K19 (21, 23) Hand sts, pm, ssk (next Hand st with first Thumb st), k14 Thumb sts, k2tog (last Thumb st with next Hand st), pm, knit to end—54 (58, 62) sts.

Work 2 rnds even.

SHAPE THUMB GUSSET

Decrease Rnd: Knit to marker, sm, ssk, knit to 2 sts before marker, k2tog, sm, knit to end—2 sts decreased.

Repeat Decrease Rnd every third rnd 5 times— 42 (46, 50) sts remain.

Next Rnd: Knit to marker, remove marker, [ssk] 0 (1, 1) time(s), k4 (2, 0), [k2tog] 0 (0, 1) time(s), remove marker, knit to end—42 (45, 48) sts remain.

CUFF

Work Rnds 1–4 of Left Cuff Pattern 4 times. Loosely BO all sts in pattern.

RIGHT MITTEN

Work as for Left Mitten to end of Thumb Gusset shaping.

CUFF

Work Rnds 1–4 of Right Cuff Pattern 4 times. Loosely BO all sts in pattern.

FINISHING

Weave in ends, using tails to close gaps at base of Thumb. Block as desired.

STITCH PATTERN

RIGHT CUFF PATTERN (SEE CHART)
(multiple of 3 sts; 4-rnd repeat)
RND 1: *K2, p1; repeat from * to end.
RND 2: *RC, p1; repeat from * to end.
RNDS 3 AND 4: Repeat Rnd 1.
Repeat Rnds 1–4 for Right Cuff Pattern.

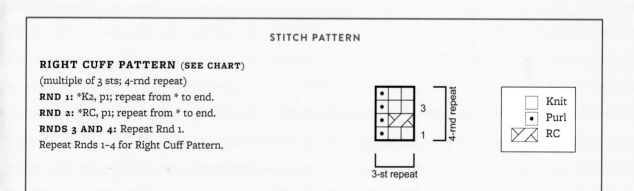

Stash-Busting Stripes

Go shopping in your yarn stash for odds and ends of yarn to knit these fun stripes. Just finished a multicolor sweater? Use the leftovers to make coordinating mittens! Follow the stripe sequence for the look shown, or make up your own. Stash-busting mittens don't even have to match each other to be a pair.

SIZES
Woman's Medium (Woman's X-Large/Man's Medium, Man's Large)

FINISHED MEASUREMENTS
7½ (8½, 9½)" [19 (21.5, 24) cm] hand circumference

8½ (9½, 9½)" [21.5 (24, 24) cm] long, including edge and cuff

YARN
Medium Weight

Ístex Léttlopi [100% new Icelandic wool; 109 yards (100 meters)/1¾ ounces (50 grams)]: Approximately 25 yards (23 meters) each #0054 Light Ash Heather (**A**), #0005 Black Heather (**B**), #1404 Glacier Blue Heather (**C**), #1406 Spring Green Heather (**D**), #1410 Orange (**E**), #1408 Light Red Heather (**F**), #9423 Lagoon Heather (**G**), and #1411 Sun Yellow (**H**)

NEEDLES
One set double-pointed needles, or other needle(s) for working a small circumference in the round, size US 8 (5 mm)

One set double-pointed needles, or other needle(s) for working a small circumference in the round, size US 7 (4.5 mm)

Change needle size if necessary to obtain correct gauge.

NOTIONS
Stitch markers; waste yarn

GAUGE
19 sts and 26 rnds = 4" (10 cm) in St st on larger needles

NOTES
These mittens are worked in the round from the bottom up. All reverse stockinette (purl) rounds are worked on smaller needles to keep tension even.

STRIPE PATTERN
See page 132

COMPONENTS

CORRUGATED RIB, PAGE 34

WESTERN GUSSET THUMB, PAGE 43

SPIRAL TOP, PAGE 46

With B, knit 7 rnds.
With E, knit 3 rnds.
With H, knit 2 rnds.
With A, knit 1 rnd; with smaller needle(s), purl 1 rnd.
Change to larger needle(s).
With H, knit 2 rnds.
With D, knit 2 rnds.
With F, knit 5 rnds.
With A, knit 1 rnd; with smaller needle(s), purl 1 rnd.
Change to larger needle(s).
With G, knit 3 rnds.
With C, knit 5 rnds.

With A, knit 1 rnd; with smaller needle(s), purl 1 rnd.
Change to larger needle(s).
With B, knit 3 rnds.
With A, knit 1 rnd; with smaller needle(s), purl 1 rnd.
Change to larger needle(s).
With E, knit 6 rnds.
With H, knit 3 rnds.
With D, knit 3 rnds.
With A, knit 1 rnd; with smaller needle(s), purl 1 rnd.
Change to larger needles.
With F, knit all remaining rnds.

MITTENS

EDGE

With F and larger needle(s), CO 36 (40, 44) sts. Join for working in the rnd, being careful not to twist sts; pm for beginning of rnd.
Knit 7 rnds.

CUFF

Next Rnd: *K2 with G, k2 with C; repeat from * to end.
Next Rnd: *K2 with G, p2 with C; repeat from * to end.
Repeat last rnd 5 times.

SHAPE THUMB GUSSET

Change to Stripe Pattern.
Set-Up Rnd: Work 18 (20, 22) sts, pm, work 1 st, pm, work to end.
Increase Rnd 1: M1, work to marker, sm, M1R, work 1 st, M1L, sm, work to end—39 (43, 47) sts. Work 2 rnds even.
Increase Rnd 2: Work to marker, sm, M1R, work to marker, M1L, sm, work to end—2 sts increased.
Repeat Increase Rnd 2 every third rnd 4 (4, 5) times—49 (53, 59) sts.
Next Rnd: Work to marker, remove marker, place 13 (13, 15) Thumb Gusset sts on waste yarn, remove marker, [M1] 0 (0, 1) time(s), work to end—36 (40, 45) sts remain.

HAND

Work even until piece measures approximately 6½ (7¼, 7½)" [16.5 (18.5, 19) cm] from bottom of rolled edge, or to approximately 2 (2¼, 2)" [5 (5.5, 5) cm] less than desired Mitten length.

SHAPE MITTEN TOP

Set-Up Rnd: *Work 9 (10, 9) sts, pm; repeat from * to end.

Decrease Rnd: *Work to 2 sts before marker, k2tog; repeat from * to end—4 (4, 5) sts decreased.

Repeat Decrease Rnd every other rnd 7 (8, 7) times—4 (4, 5) sts remain.

Break yarn, leaving a long tail. Thread tail through remaining sts, pull tight, and fasten off to WS.

THUMB

Transfer Thumb Gusset sts to larger needle(s); rejoin yarn.

Continue in Stripe Pattern.

Next Rnd: M1, work to end—14 (14, 16) sts.

Work even until Thumb measures approximately 1¾" (4.5 cm), or to ½" (12 mm) less than desired Thumb length.

SHAPE THUMB TOP

Next Rnd: *K2tog; repeat from * to end— 7 (7, 8) sts remain.

Next Rnd: *K2tog; repeat from * to last 1 (1, 0) st(s), k1 (1, 0)—4 sts remain.

Break yarn, leaving a long tail. Thread tail through remaining sts, pull tight, and fasten off to WS.

FINISHING

Weave in ends, using tails to close gaps at base of Thumb. Block as desired, allowing Edge to roll.

Winter Garden

Loved in cold climates around the world for their wind- and water-resistant qualities, fulled mittens are easy to make and delightful to wear. The directions below will yield mittens that are intentionally large, to be shrunk to size with hot water and agitation. Add the optional simple embroidery for a bright and cheery finish.

SIZES
Woman's Medium (Woman's Large, Woman's X-Large)

FINISHED MEASUREMENTS
7½ (8, 8½)″ [19 (20.5, 21.5) cm] hand circumference, after fulling

8½ (9, 9¼)″ [21.5 (23, 23.5) cm] long, including hem and cuff, after fulling

9¼ (10, 10¾)″ [23.5 (25.5, 27.5) cm] hand circumference, before fulling

10 (10¾, 11)″ [25.5 (27.5, 28) cm] long, including hem and cuff, before fulling

YARN
Bulky Weight

Ístex Álafosslopi [100% new Icelandic wool; 109 yards (100 meters)/3½ ounces (100 grams)]: 2 skeins #054 Light Ash Heather (**MC**)

CYC #0 Lace

Ístex Einband [100% wool; 273 yards (250 meters)/1¾ ounces (50 grams)]: 1 skein each #1766 Orange (**A**), #9268 Lime (**B**), and #1768 Pink (**C**)

NEEDLES
One set double-pointed needles, or other needle(s) for working a small circumference in the round, size US 8 (5 mm)

Change needle size if necessary to obtain correct gauge.

NOTIONS
Stitch markers; waste yarn; tapestry needle; crewel embroidery needle

GAUGE
12 sts and 16 rnds = 4″ (10 cm) in St st, before fulling

15 sts and 19 rnds = 4″ (10 cm) in St st, after fulling

NOTE
These mittens are worked in the round from the bottom up.

COMPONENTS

WESTERN
GUSSET
THUMB,
PAGE 43

SYMMETRICAL
TOP,
PAGE 48

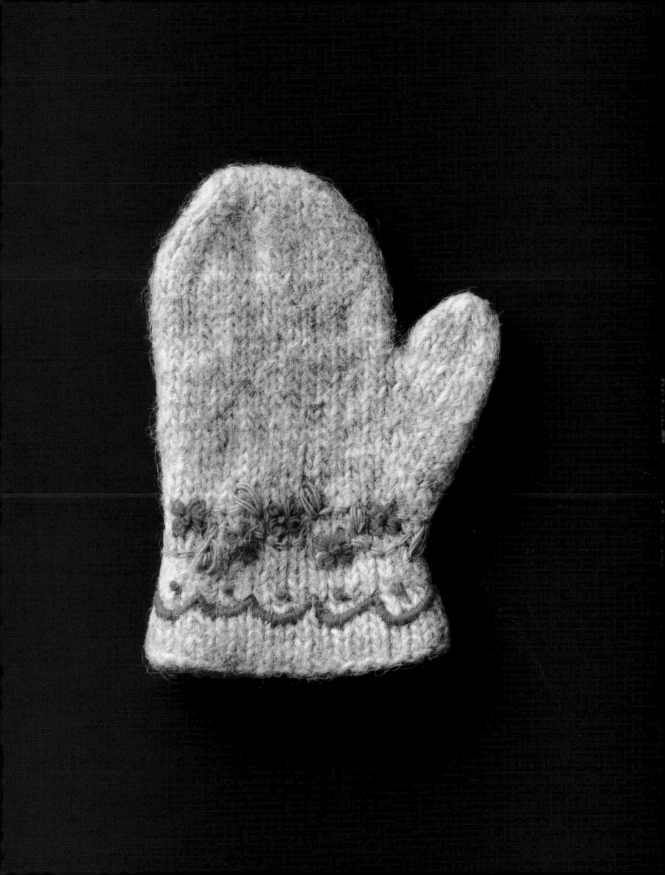

MITTENS

HEM

With MC, CO 28 (30, 32) sts. Join for working in the rnd, being careful not to twist sts; pm for beginning of rnd.

Knit 5 rnds.

Turning Rnd: Purl.

Knit 5 rnds.

Fold hem to WS along Turning Rnd.

Next Rnd: *Insert left needle into first CO st and k2tog (CO st and next st on needle); repeat from * for each CO st—28 (30, 32) sts remain.

CUFF

Next Rnd: M1, knit to end—29 (31, 33) sts.

Knit 5 rnds.

SHAPE THUMB GUSSET

Set-Up Rnd: K14 (15, 16), pm, k1, pm, knit to end.

Increase Rnd: Knit to marker, sm, M1R, knit to marker, M1L, sm, knit to end—2 sts increased.

Repeat Increase Rnd every third rnd 3 (4, 5) times—37 (41, 45) sts.

Next Rnd: Knit to marker, remove marker, place 9 (11, 13) Thumb Gusset sts on waste yarn, remove marker, knit to end—28 (30, 32) sts remain.

HAND

Work even until piece measures approximately 8 (8¾, 9)" [20.5 (22, 23) cm] from Turning Rnd, or to approximately 2" (5 cm) less than desired Mitten length before fulling.

SHAPE MITTEN TOP

Set-Up Rnd: K14 (15, 16), pm, knit to end.

Decrease Rnd: *K1, ssk, work to 3 sts before marker, k2tog, k1; repeat from * once—4 sts decreased.

Repeat Decrease Rnd every other rnd 3 times—12 (14, 16) sts remain.

Break yarn, leaving a 16" (40.5 cm) tail.

Using Kitchener st (see *Special Techniques*, page 154), graft Mitten Top.

THUMB

Transfer Thumb Gusset sts to needle(s); rejoin MC.

Increase Rnd: M1, knit to end—10 (12, 14) sts.

Join for working in the rnd; pm for beginning of rnd.

Work even until Thumb measures approximately 1" (2.5 cm) less than desired Thumb length.

SHAPE THUMB TOP

Decrease Rnd: *K1, k2tog; repeat from * to last 1 (0, 2) st(s), k1 (0, 2)—7 (8, 10) sts remain.

Knit 1 rnd.

Decrease Rnd: *K2tog; repeat from * to last 1 (0, 0) st(s), k1 (0, 0)—4 (4, 5) sts remain.

Break yarn, leaving a long tail. Thread tail through remaining sts, pull tight, and fasten off to WS.

FINISHING

Weave in ends, using tails to close gaps at base of Thumb. Full Mittens in washing machine using a small load, hot water, and a small amount of soap. Check Mittens frequently and remove when the desired size is reached. **Note:** *Mittens should be fulled, not felted (you should still be able to see individual knit sts).*

EMBROIDERY

Referring to diagram at right, work embroidery with a sharp-tipped crewel needle, threaded double, as follows.

Swags: With A, work 1 long foundation st for each swag (Figure 1A).
Cover each swag with short satin sts (Figure 1B).

French Knots: With C, work 1 French knot centered on each swag (Figure 2).

Vine: With B, work backstitches in a serpentine pattern as shown (Figure 3).

Flowers: With C, work 4 filled lazy daisy petal sts for each flower (Figures 4a–4c), alternating each side of the vine.
With A, work 1 French knot in the center of each flower (Figure 4).

Leaves: With B, work elongated filled lazy daisy stitches (Figures 5a–5c), alternating on either side of the vine (Figure 5).

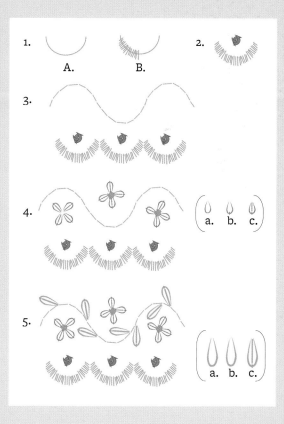

Opera

Fashionable ladies have worn long gloves on formal occasions for centuries. Only the very longest, reaching well above the elbows, may be called opera gloves. This pair omits the fingers so you won't need to remove them in order to text your driver. Wear your diamond bracelets on the outside, and don't forget your tiara. We're not savages, after all.

SIZE
Woman's Large

FINISHED MEASUREMENTS
8″ (20.5 cm) hand circumference

19½″ (49.5 cm) long, including cuff

YARN
Super Fine Weight

Anzula Nebula [86% superwash merino/ 14% sparkling stellina; 400 yards (365 meters)/ 4 ounces (114 grams)]: 1 skein Mariana

NEEDLES
One set double-pointed needles, or other needle(s) for working a small circumference in the round, size US 3 (3.25 mm)

One set double-pointed needles, or other needle(s) for working a small circumference in the round, size US 4 (3.5 mm)

Change needle size if necessary to obtain correct gauge.

NOTIONS
Stitch markers; waste yarn

GAUGE
36 sts and 37 rnds = 4″ (10 cm) in 2x2 Rib on smaller needles, stretched as worn

NOTES
These mitts are worked in the round from the lace cuff up. One size is given, which fits bicep up to 12″ (30.5 cm). You may work Cuff and Hand Patterns from text or charts.

The sample used all of one skein of yarn. Consider purchasing an extra skein as insurance.

STITCH PATTERNS
See page 141

COMPONENTS

WESTERN GUSSET THUMB, PAGE 43

MITTS

CUFF

Using larger needle(s) and Tubular CO (see *Special Techniques*, page 155) or CO of your choice, CO 84 sts. Join for working in the rnd, being careful not to twist sts; pm for beginning of rnd.

Work 1 rnd of 1x1 Rib.

Change to smaller needle(s).

Knit 1 rnd.

Work Rnds 1–11 of Cuff Pattern—72 sts remain.

Knit 1 rnd.

Purl 1 rnd.

ARM

Work in 2x2 Rib until piece measures 13½" (34.5 cm) from purl rnd.

SHAPE THUMB GUSSET

Set-Up Rnd: Work to last 2 sts, pm, p2.

Increase Rnd: Work to marker, sm, yo, work to end, yo, sm—2 sts increased.

Repeat Increase Rnd every third rnd 7 times, working new sts into 2x2 Rib—88 sts.

Next Rnd: M1P, work to marker, remove marker, place 18 Thumb Gusset sts on waste yarn, M1P—72 sts remain.

HAND

Work in pattern for approximately ¾" (2 cm).

Purl 1 rnd.

Work Rnds 1–7 of Hand Pattern.

With larger needle(s), work 1 rnd of 1x1 Rib.

BO using Tubular BO (see *Special Techniques*, page 155), or in pattern using your preferred BO.

THUMB

Transfer Thumb Gusset sts to smaller needle(s); rejoin yarn.

Next Rnd: Pick up and knit 1 st, work in pattern to end, pick up and knit 1 st—20 sts.

Work in pattern until Thumb measures approximately ¾" (2 cm).

With larger needle(s), work 1 rnd of 1x1 Rib.

BO using Tubular BO, or in pattern using your preferred BO.

FINISHING

Weave in ends, using tails to close gaps at base of Thumb. Steam lightly to block, pinning out points on Cuff.

STITCH PATTERNS

1X1 RIB

(even number of sts; 1-rnd repeat)

ALL RNDS: *K1, p1; repeat from * to end.

2X2 RIB

(multiple of 4 sts; 1-rnd repeat)

ALL RNDS: *K2, p2; repeat from * to end.

CUFF PATTERN (SEE CHART)

(14-st repeat; decreases to 12-st repeat)

RND 1: K6, sk2p, k5—12 sts remain.

RND 2 AND ALL EVEN-NUMBERED RNDS: Knit.

RND 3: K1, yo, k4, sk2p, k4, yo.

RND 5: K2, yo, k3, sk2p, k3, yo, k1.

RND 7: K3, yo, k2, sk2p, k2, yo, k2.

RND 9: K4, yo, k1, sk2p, k1, yo, k3.

RND 11: K5, yo, sk2p, yo, k4.

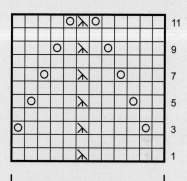

14-st repeat; decreases to 12-st repeat

HAND PATTERN (SEE CHART)

(6-st repeat)

RND 1 AND ALL ODD-NUMBERED RNDS: Knit.

RND 2: Yo, k1, sk2p, k1, yo, k1.

RND 4: K1, yo, sk2p, yo, k2.

RND 6: K2, yo, ssk, k2.

RND 7: Knit.

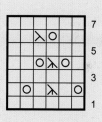

6-st repeat

	Knit
O	Yo
⧄	Ssk
⅄	Sk2p

Freya's Minions

The Norse goddess Freya was said to travel with a retinue of dragonflies who waited at the ready to do her bidding. Until you're that well waited-upon, you can wear these. And dream.

SIZE
Man's Large

FINISHED MEASUREMENTS
9″ (23 cm) hand circumference

10″ (25.5 cm) long, including hem and cuff

YARN
Fine Weight

Swans Island All American, Sport [100% USA rambouillet wool; 185 yards (169 meters)/1⅖ ounces (40 grams)]: 1 skein each of #AAS215 Nasturtium (**MC**), #AAS211 Hibiscus (**CC1**), #AAS208 Fuchsia (**CC2**), and #AAS224 Fern (**CC3**)

NEEDLES
One set double-pointed needles, or other needle(s) for working a small circumference in the round, size US 2 (2.75 mm)

Change needle size if necessary to obtain correct gauge.

NOTIONS
Stitch markers; waste yarn; tapestry needle

GAUGE
32 sts and 35 rnds = 4″ (10 cm) in charted pattern

NOTES
These mittens are worked in the round from the bottom up.

One size is given; the size may be adjusted by working at a firmer or looser gauge. See the worksheet on page 19 for instructions.

COMPONENTS

KNITTED
PICOT HEM,
PAGE 29

SCANDINAVIAN
GUSSET
THUMB,
PAGE 41

POINTED
TOP,
PAGE 45

LEFT MITTEN

HEM

With CC3, CO 60 sts. Join for working in the rnd, being careful not to twist sts; pm for beginning of rnd.

Knit 6 rnds.

Picot Rnd: *P2tog, yo; repeat from * to end.

Knit 1 rnd.

Change to MC.

Knit 5 rnds.

Fold hem to WS along Picot Rnd.

Next Rnd: *Insert left needle into first CO st and k2tog (CO st and next st on needle); repeat from * for each CO st—60 sts remain.

CUFF AND THUMB GUSSET

Work Rnds 1–34 of Left Mitten chart—72 sts.

Next Rnd (Rnd 35 of chart): Work 19 sts in pattern, place next 17 Thumb Gusset sts on waste yarn, CO 17 sts in pattern, work to end.

HAND AND MITTEN TOP

Work Rnds 36–83 of chart—4 sts remain.

Break yarns, leaving long tails.

To close Mitten Top, remove needle(s) from last 4 sts.

Use the tip of the tapestry needle or a crochet hook to pull center back st through center front st and thread MC tail through center back st.

Pull right side st through left side st and thread CC1 tail through right side st.

Fasten off to WS.

THUMB

Transfer 17 Thumb Gusset sts to needle(s); rejoin yarns.

Next Rnd: Work Thumb chart across 17 sts, pick up and knit 15 sts through CO edge of Palm according to last 15 sts of chart—32 sts.

Join for working in the rnd; pm for beginning of rnd.

Work Rnds 2–25 of Thumb chart—4 sts remain.

Close Thumb Top as for Mitten Top.

RIGHT MITTEN

Work as for Left Mitten to end of Hem.

CUFF AND THUMB GUSSET

Work Rnds 1–34 of Right Mitten chart—72 sts.

Next Rnd (Rnd 35 of chart): Work 36 sts in pattern, place next 17 Thumb Gusset sts on waste yarn, CO 17 sts in pattern, work to end.

Complete as for Left Mitten.

FINISHING

Weave in ends, using tails to close gaps at base of Thumb. Block as desired.

THUMB

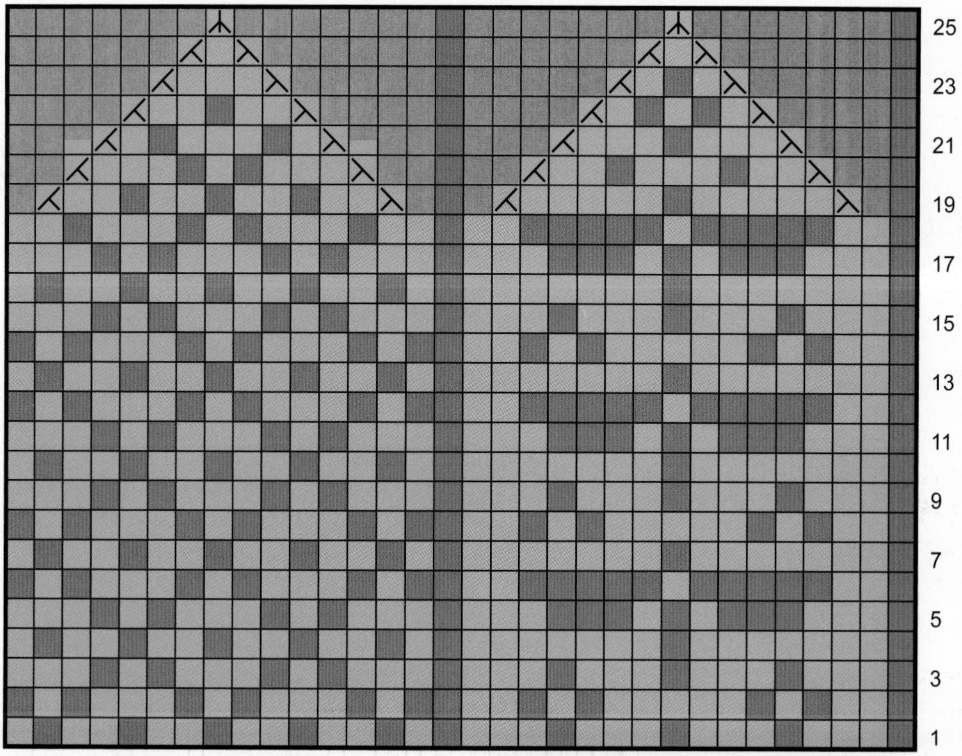

- MC
- CC1
- No st
- K2tog
- Ssk
- S2kp2

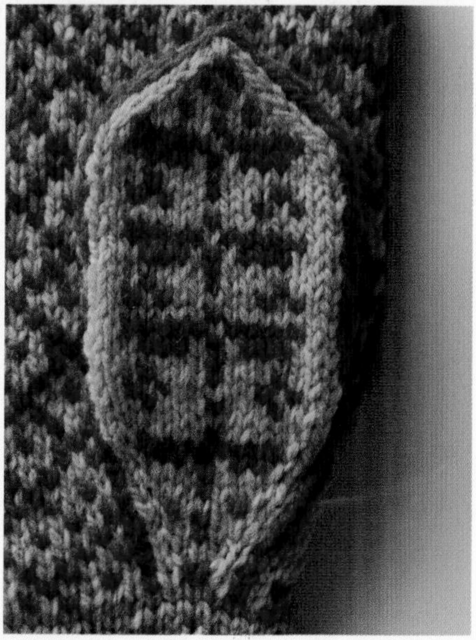

LEFT MITTEN

83
81
79
77
75
73
71
69
67
65
63
61
59
57
55
53
51
49
47
45
43
41
39
37
35
33
31
29
27
25
23
21
19
17
15
13
11
9
7
5
3
1

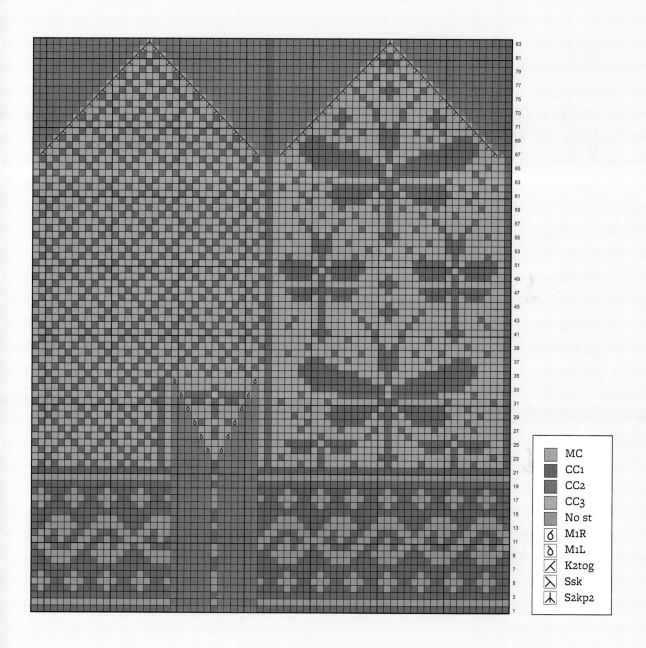

Steampunkery

Here's a flight of fancy with old-fashioned style for your next modern-day adventure. It's a great example of how you can make two completely different fabrics from the same yarn, using the magic of gauge. The main mitt is worked with a doubled strand of laceweight yarn, equivalent to fingering weight. Knit on small needles, it's a stable but soft and stretchy hand fabric. The sash embellishment is worked with a single strand of the same yarn on much larger needles to achieve a sheer, lofty fabric.

SIZES
Woman's Medium (Woman's Large, Woman's X-Large)

FINISHED MEASUREMENTS
7½ (8, 8½)" [19 (20.5, 21.5) cm] hand circumference
6 (6¼, 6½)" [15 (16, 16.5) cm] long, including cuff

YARN
Lace Weight

Anzula Wash My Lace [100% superwash merino; 980 yards (896 meters)/ 4 ounces (114 grams)]: 1 skein Plum

NEEDLES
One set double-pointed needles, or other needle(s) for working a small circumference in the round, size US 1 (2.25 mm)

One set double-pointed needles, or other needle(s) for working a small circumference in the round, size US 9 (5.5 mm)

Change needle size if necessary to obtain correct gauge.

NOTIONS
Stitch markers; waste yarn; tapestry needle; two 1½" × 1¼" (4 × 3 cm) buckles

GAUGE
32 sts and 44 rnds = 4" (10 cm) in St st with 2 strands of yarn held together on smaller needle(s)

17 sts and 23 rows = 4" (10 cm) in St st with 1 strand of yarn on larger needle(s)

NOTES
These mitts are worked from the bottom up in the round. The sash detail is picked up and knit from the mitt and worked in rows.

Work with 2 strands of yarn held together for the mitt, and 1 strand of yarn for the sash.

STITCH PATTERN

1X1 RIB
(even number of sts; 1-rnd repeat)
ALL RNDS: *K1, p1; repeat from * to end.

COMPONENTS

PALM
GUSSET
THUMB,
PAGE 40

LEFT MITT

CUFF

Using smaller needle(s), 2 strands of yarn held together, and Tubular CO (see *Special Techniques*, page 155) or CO of your choice, CO 60 (64, 68) sts. Join for working in the rnd, being careful not to twist sts; pm for beginning of rnd.

Work in 1x1 Rib for 2" (5 cm).

SHAPE PALM GUSSET

Set-Up Rnd: K10 (11, 12), pm, knit to last 10 (11, 12) sts, pm, knit to end.

Increase Rnd: Work to marker, sm, M1L, knit to marker, M1R, sm, knit to end—2 Hand sts increased.

Repeat Increase Rnd every third rnd 9 (10, 11) times—80 (86, 92) sts.

Work 1 rnd even.

Next Rnd: Knit to second marker, remove marker, place 20 (22, 24) Thumb sts on waste yarn, sm (this now marks beginning of rnd)—60 (64, 68) sts remain.

HAND

Work even until piece measures approximately 5½ (5¾, 6)" [14 (14.5, 15) cm] from CO, or to ½" (12 mm) less than desired Mitt length.

Work 6 rnds of 1x1 Rib.

Using Tubular BO (see *Special Techniques*, page 155), BO all sts.

THUMB

Transfer Thumb sts to needle(s); rejoin 2 strands of yarn held together.

Join for working in the rnd; pm for beginning of rnd.

Knit 3 rnds, or until Thumb measures approximately ¼" (6 mm) less than desired Thumb length.

Work 3 rnds of 1x1 Rib.

Using Tubular BO, BO all sts.

SASH

With RS facing, 1 strand of yarn, and larger needle(s), beginning at base of top Rib, pick up and knit 12 sts between Rib and Thumb.

Next Row (WS): *K1-f/b; repeat from * to end—24 sts.

Work in St st in rows until piece measures 6" (15 cm), ending with a WS row.

Work 6 rows of Garter st.

BO all sts.

RIGHT MITT

Work as for Left Mitt to end of Thumb.

SASH

With RS facing, 1 strand of yarn, and larger needle(s), beginning at crook of Thumb, pick up and knit 12 sts between Thumb and base of top Rib.

Next Row (WS): *K1-f/b; repeat from * to end—24 sts.

Work in St st in rows until piece measures 6" (15 cm), ending with a WS row.

Work 6 rows of Garter st.

BO all sts.

FINISHING

Weave in ends, using tails to close gaps at base of Thumb. With yarn, sew buckle to back of hand at lower edge above cuff, as shown. Gather sash and thread through buckle, adjusting fullness.

Tiny Crackers

Do you remember a time when you were so small you didn't know how to use your thumbs? Me either, but if you're lucky, at some point you'll meet a person that size. If you're really lucky, you'll get to watch them learn how. Until they do, help keep those wee hands cozy with these thumbless mittens, inspired by every little one's favorite tiny fish crackers.

SIZE
Baby

FINISHED MEASUREMENTS
4½" (11.5 cm) hand circumference

4" (10 cm) long, including cuff and tail

YARN
Super Fine Weight

Blue Moon Fiber Arts Socks That Rock Lightweight [100% superwash merino wool; 405 yards (370 meters)/5⅛ ounces (146 grams)]: 1 skein Cozy Fierce and Dirty Orange; approximately 2 yards (1.8 meters) Dark Brown for embroidery

NEEDLES
One set double-pointed needles, or other needle(s) for working a small circumference in the round, size US 2 (2.75 mm)

One set double-pointed needles, or other needle(s) for working a small circumference in the round, size US 1 (2.25 mm)

Change needle size if necessary to obtain correct gauge.

NOTIONS
Stitch markers; tapestry needle

GAUGE
28 sts and 40 rnds = 4" (10 cm) in St st on larger needle(s)

NOTES
These mittens are worked from the top down in the round. One size is given; the size may be adjusted by working at a firmer or looser gauge. See the worksheet on page 19 for instructions.

STITCH PATTERN

1X1 RIB

(even number of sts; 1-rnd repeat)

ALL RNDS: *K1, p1; repeat from * to end.

COMPONENTS

TOP-DOWN INCREASED, PAGE 48

MITTENS

SHAPE MITTEN TOP

With larger needle(s) and using Judy's Magic CO (see *Special Techniques*, page 154), CO 20 sts. Join for working in the rnd; pm for beginning of rnd.

Set-Up Rnd: K10, pm, k10.

Increase Rnd: *K1, M1R, knit to 1 st before marker, M1L, k1; repeat from * once—4 sts increased.

Repeat Increase Rnd every other rnd twice—32 sts.

Work even until piece measures approximately 2½" (6.5 cm) from CO.

CUFF

Change to smaller needle(s).

Work approximately ¾" (2 cm) of 1x1 Rib.

TAIL

Change to larger needle(s).

Increase Rnd: *K8, M1L, pm; repeat from * to end—36 sts.

Shaping Rnd: *Knit to 2 sts before marker, s2kp2 (removing marker), pm, knit to 1 st before marker, M1R, k1, sm, M1L; repeat from * once.

Repeat Shaping Rnd every other rnd twice.

Knit 1 rnd.

Work 1 rnd of 1x1 Rib.

Loosely BO all sts in pattern.

FINISHING

Weave in ends. Steam lightly to block, pinning out points on tail. Embroider mouth and eye on both sides of Mitten as shown below.

French Knot

Backstitch

CABLE CO: Make a loop (using a slipknot) with the working yarn and place it on the left-hand needle (first st CO), knit into slipknot, draw up a loop but do not drop st from left-hand needle; place new loop on left-hand needle; *insert the tip of the right-hand needle into the space between the last 2 sts on the left-hand needle and draw up a loop; place the loop on the left-hand needle. Repeat from * for remaining sts to be CO, or for casting on at the end of a row in progress.

CROCHET CHAIN: Make a slipknot and place it on crochet hook. Holding tail end of yarn in left hand, *take hook under ball end of yarn from front to back; draw yarn on hook back through previous st on hook to form new st. Repeat from * to desired number of sts or length of chain.

JUDY'S MAGIC CO: Worked with two needles. Make a slipknot and place the loop around one of the needles. The anchor loop counts as the first st. Hold the two needles together, with the needle that the yarn is attached to toward the top. This needle is needle #2 and the other needle is needle #1. In your other hand, hold the yarn so that the tail goes over your index finger and the working yarn (the yarn that leads to the ball) goes over your thumb. (This is opposite from how the yarn is usually held for a long-tail CO.) *Bring the tip of needle #1 over the strand of yarn on your finger, then around and under the yarn and back up, making a loop around needle #1. Pull the loop snug, but not tight, around the needle. Bring needle #2 over the yarn tail on your thumb, around and under the yarn and back up, making a loop around needle #2. Pull the loop snug around the needle. There are now two sts on needle #2: the st you just CO plus the anchor loop. The top yarn strand always wraps around needle #1 (the bottom needle), and the bottom yarn strand always wraps around needle #2 (the top needle). Repeat from * until all sts are CO, ending with a loop around needle #1.

KITCHENER STITCH: Using a blunt tapestry needle, thread a length of yarn approximately four times the length of the section to be joined. Hold the pieces to be joined wrong sides together, with the needles holding the sts parallel, both ends pointing to the right.

Working from right to left, insert tapestry needle into first st on front needle as if to purl, pull yarn through, leaving st on needle; insert tapestry needle into first st on back needle as if to knit, pull yarn through, leaving st on needle; *insert tapestry needle into first st on front needle as if to knit, pull yarn through, remove st from needle; insert tapestry needle into next st on front needle as if to purl, pull yarn through, leave st on needle; insert tapestry needle into first st on back needle as if to purl, pull yarn through, remove st from needle; insert tapestry needle into next st on back needle as if to knit, pull yarn through, leave st on needle. Repeat from *, working 3 or 4 sts at a time, then adjust tension to match the pieces being joined. When 1 st remains on each needle, pass through last 2 sts to fasten off, and weave in end.

LONG-TAIL (THUMB) CO: Leaving tail with about 1" (2.5 cm) of yarn for each st to be cast on, make a slipknot in the yarn and place it on the right-hand needle, with the tail to the front and the working end to the back. Insert the thumb and forefinger of your left hand between the strands of yarn so that the working end is around your forefinger and the tail end is around your thumb "slingshot" fashion; *insert the tip of the right-hand needle into the front loop on the thumb. Bring the needle over the strand of yarn coming from the forefinger, catch the yarn, and draw it through the loop on your thumb; remove your thumb from the loop and pull on the working yarn to tighten the new st on the right-hand needle; return your thumb and forefinger to their original positions, and repeat from * for remaining sts to be CO.

MAGIC LOOP: It is best to work Magic Loop on a 32" (80 cm) long or longer circular needle with a flexible cable. Divide the stitches roughly in half and fold the piece flat, holding the two halves together, with the needles at the right. At the halfway point (on the left opposite the loose cables), pull the cable out between two stitches until you have a large loop. Pull the loop until the stitches are at both needle tips, then pull the back needle out until the back stitches are on the cable and you have a loop large enough to allow you to work across the stitches on the front needle with the back needle; you will still have the loop at the halfway point on the left side of the piece. Work across the stitches on the front needle until you get to the loop on the left side. Turn the piece so that the front needle becomes the back needle; slide the stitches on the new front needle to the needle tip, and pull the back needle out until it is long enough to work the stitches on the front needle.

PROVISIONAL (CROCHET CHAIN) CO: Using a crochet hook and smooth yarn (crochet cotton or ravel cord used for machine knitting), work a crochet chain with a few more chains than the number of sts needed; fasten off. If desired, tie a knot on the fastened-off end to mark the end that you will be unraveling from later. Turn the chain over; with a needle 1 size smaller than required for piece and working yarn, starting a few chains in from the beginning of the chain, pick up and knit one st in each bump at the back of the chain, leaving any extra chains at the end unworked. Change to needle size required for project on first row. When ready to work the live sts, unravel the chain by loosening the fastened-off end and "unzipping" the chain, placing the live sts on a spare needle.

THREE-NEEDLE BO: Place the sts to be joined onto two same-size needles; hold the pieces to be joined with the right sides facing each other and the needles parallel, both pointing to the right. Holding both needles in your left hand, using working yarn and a third needle same size or one size larger, insert third needle into first st on front needle, then into first st on back needle; knit these 2 sts together; *knit next st from each needle together (2 sts on right-hand needle); pass first st over second st to BO 1 st. Repeat from * until 1 st remains on third needle and no sts on other two needles; cut yarn and fasten off.

TUBULAR BO: Row 1: *K1, slip 1 purlwise wyif; repeat from * to end.
Repeat Row 1 once. Divide sts onto 2 needles as follows: *Slip 1 purlwise to front needle, slip 1 purlwise to back needle; repeat from * to end. Using Kitchener st, graft sts.

TUBULAR CO: Allow ½" (12 mm) of tail for each st to be CO, make a slipknot, and place slipknot onto right needle (counts as 1 st). Hold yarn going to ball in right hand and tail in left hand.

A. Holding st on needle with thumb of left hand, pass ball strand under needle to front and over needle to back.
B. Holding st with thumb of right hand, pass tail over needle from back to front.
C. Holding sts with thumb of left hand, cross ball strand at front over tail and under needle to back.
D. Holding sts with thumb of right hand, pass tail over needle from back to front.
E. Holding sts with thumb of left hand, pass ball strand under needle to front and over needle to back.
F. Holding sts with thumb of right hand, pass tail over ball strand from front to back, then under needle and to front again—2 sts CO (plus slipknot).
Repeat steps A–F until 1 fewer st than the required number of sts has been CO. Holding last st with thumb, bring tail over needle from back to front, then tie tail and ball strand in a knot under needle.
Row 1: K1, *slip 1 purlwise wyif, k1-tbl; repeat from * to last st, slip 1 purlwise wyif.
Row 2: *K1, slip 1 purlwise wyif; repeat from * to end.

WORKING IN THE ROUND ON TWO CIRCULAR NEEDLES: If your stitches are not already on two circular needles, divide them evenly (or as directed) between the needles. Hold the needles so that Needle 2 is in the back, with the working yarn at the right. Slide the stitches on Needle 2 to the cable of the needle; slide the stitches on Needle 1 to the tip of the needle closest to the working yarn. With the free end of Needle 1, work across the Needle 1 stitches as instructed, making sure to pull the yarn snug when working the first stitch, so that you do not have a gap between it and the last stitch on Needle 2. Once these stitches have been worked, slide the needle so that the stitches are on the cable of the needle. Turn the work so that Needle 1 is now in the back, with the working yarn at the right. Slide the stitches on Needle 2 to the tip closest to the working yarn. With the free end of Needle 2, work across the Needle 2 stitches as instructed, making sure to pull the yarn snug when working the first stitch. Continue working in this manner, always working with only one needle at a time, working the stitches on the needle with the other end of the same needle, and leaving the other needle hanging free.

BO: Bind off

CC: Contrasting color

CN: Cable needle

CO: Cast on

K1-F/B: Knit into the front loop and back loop of the same stitch to increase 1 stitch

K1-F/B/F: Knit into the front loop, back loop, and front loop of the same stitch to increase 2 stitches

K1-F/B/F/B: Knit into the front loop, back loop, front loop, and back loop of the same stitch to increase 3 stitches

K1-F/B/F/B/F: Knit into the front loop, back loop, front loop, back loop, and front loop of the same stitch to increase 4 stitches

K1-TBL: Knit 1 stitch through the back loop

K2TOG: Knit 2 stitches together

K: Knit

M1 OR M1L (MAKE 1–LEFT SLANTING): With the tip of the left-hand needle inserted from front to back, lift the strand between the 2 needles onto the left-hand needle; knit the strand through the back loop to increase 1 stitch

M1P OR M1PR (MAKE 1 PURLWISE–RIGHT SLANTING): With the tip of the left-hand needle inserted from back to front, lift the strand between the 2 needles onto the left-hand needle; purl the strand through the front loop to increase 1 stitch

M1R (MAKE 1–RIGHT SLANTING): With the tip of the left-hand needle inserted from back to front, lift the strand between the 2 needles onto the left-hand needle; knit the strand through the front loop to increase 1 stitch

MC: Main Color

P2TOG: Purl 2 stitches together

P: Purl

PM: Place marker

RND(S): Round(s)

RS: Right side

S2KP2 (DOUBLE DECREASE): Slip the next 2 stitches together to the right-hand needle as if to knit 2 together, k1, pass the 2 slipped stitches over

SK2P (DOUBLE DECREASE): Slip the next stitch knitwise to the right-hand needle, k2tog, pass the slipped stitch over the stitch from the k2tog

SM: Slip marker

SSK (SLIP, SLIP, KNIT): Slip the next 2 stitches to the right-hand needle one at a time as if to knit; return them to the left-hand needle one at a time in their new orientation; knit them together through the back loops

ST(S): Stitch(es)

ST ST: Stockinette stitch

TBL: Through the back loop

WRP-T: Wrap and turn

WS: Wrong side

WYIF: With yarn in front

YO: Yarnover

RESOURCES

ABSTRACT FIBER
www.abstractfiber.com

ANZULA LUXURY FIBERS
www.anzula.com

BLUE MOON FIBER ARTS, INC.
www.bluemoonfiberarts.com

BROWN SHEEP COMPANY, INC.
www.brownsheep.com

CASCADE YARNS
www.cascadeyarns.com

HARRISVILLE DESIGNS
www.harrisville.com

JILL DRAPER MAKES STUFF
www.etsy.com/shop/jilldrapermakesstuff

FOR LOPI YARN AND WENDY WOOL
www.handknitting.com

MADELINETOSH
www.madelinetosh.com

PLYMOUTH YARN COMPANY, INC.
www.plymouthyarn.com

RAUMA YARNS
www.theyarnguys.com

SHEEPSPOT
www.sheepspot.com

SWANS ISLAND COMPANY
www.swansislandcompany.com

ACKNOWLEDGMENTS

This book was made possible by the kind efforts of those of you who know and work with me. To my students, who asked me to write it, I offer my heartfelt thanks for the journey of discovery you led me on, and your gracious contributions of knowledge and support. For the gentle readers of my blog, please accept my deep appreciation of your daily fellowship and cheerful insistence that I find you the best answers to your questions. You all are the reason I love to play with string. Linda Roghaar, you are the lifeline in my lace. Thank you for keeping me on track and off the ledge. Cristina Garces, I deeply appreciate your vision and gentle leadership. Thank you for making a beautiful book. Many thanks also to Deb Wood and Lesley Unruh, who know the value of the visual. Without your beautiful work, I'm just a bag of yarn and words. To Karen Frisa and Sue McCain, may the readers know that your diligence is the reason they can knit these projects. I know I do. Carson Demers, you are my coworker at the water cooler, and so very much more. Blessings on you. To my family, who still have not complained that they live in a pile of books and yarn, thank you. Phillip, Lindsay, Campbell, Bailey, Paisley, and Ruby: Thank you for sitting companionably with me while I knit and ignore the laundry. I couldn't ask for more.

Editor: Cristina Garces
Designer: Deb Wood
Production Manager: Alexandra Cameron
Prop Styling: Pam Morris

Library of Congress Control Number: 2016961383

ISBN: 978-1-4197-2662-0

Printed and bound in the United States
10 9 8 7 6 5 4 3 2

Abrams books are available at special discounts when
purchased in quantity for premiums and promotions as
well as fundraising or educational use. Special editions
can also be created to specification. For details,
contact specialsales@abramsbooks.com or the address
below.

ABRAMS The Art of Books
195 Broadway, New York, NY 10007
abramsbooks.com

3 1333 04894 2906